Training Your Dog the Weatherwax Way

The Complete Guide to Selecting, Raising, and Caring for Your Canine

R. Ruddell Weatherwax

Skyhorse Publishing

Skyhorse Publishing books may be purchased in bulk at special discounts for sales promotion, corporate gifts, fund-raising, or educational purposes. Special editions can also be created to specifications. For details, contact the Special Sales Department, Skyhorse Publishing, 307 West 36th Street, 11th Floor, New York, NY 10018 or info@skyhorsepublishing.com.

Visit our website at www.skyhorsepublishing.com.

10 9 8 7 6 5 4 3 2 1

Library of Congress Cataloging-in-Publication Data is available on file.

Cover design by Daniel Brount
Cover photo by Ace Collins

Print ISBN: 978-1-5107-6343-2
Ebook ISBN: 978-1-5107-6344-9

Printed in China

CONTENTS

INTRODUCTION

I could have written this book many years ago. It crossed my mind on more than one occasion. What kept me from following through? History. I was a third-generation dog trainer with a grandfather who already had two dog training books published and a father who had filmed a dog training video. What, then, could I bring to an already crowded table? Simple. I could bring answers to the questions dog owners face every day. While the tricks for TV and movies my family taught were amazing, how many people really need to teach their dog all these things? It was then I realized my calling has always been more as a dog *behaviorist* than a *trainer*. So, as you read the following chapters, keep in mind that when I speak of "training," I'm doing so in the context of "behavior modification."

Forget for a moment that my grandfather, Rudd B. Weatherwax, not only trained seven generations of Lassie going all the way back to 1941 with the original Lassie ("Pal"), but also trained some of the earliest canine stars such as Asta, the popular terrier in the *Thin Man* movies. Rudd's roots can even be traced as far back as the silent film era when he assisted with the training of "Petey" from the earliest *Our Gang* comedies.

My father, Robert W. Weatherwax, not only assisted his father, Rudd, on the Lassie television series for eleven years, but also continued the Lassie legacy as head trainer after Rudd's death. In fact, I assisted my father as a young trainer on the 1989–91 series *The New Lassie*. It was my father who trained the first dog to travel through time (Einstein from *Back to the Future*). Between those two men alone, hundreds of dogs were trained for various TV and film roles.

Then there were my great-uncles, Frank and Jack Weatherwax. Rudd's older brother, Frank, was responsible for training numerous dogs for Hollywood, with *Old Yeller* and *A Dog of Flanders* being his most well-known canine vehicles. Can anyone forget Rudd's younger brother Jack Weatherwax's work with Toto from the classic *The Wizard of Oz*?

You can see how my own lengthy stint training dogs for TV and film could get lost in the shuffle. My credits as a trainer include such films as *Beethoven*, *K-9*, and *Dennis the Menace*. Plus, there are my TV credits, including such shows as *The Flash*, *Just the Ten of Us*, and *Married with Children*.

When I first began working for my father after serving in the Navy, he hadn't fully embraced me as a trainer. He gave me a female Briard named Betty and said, "Here, you can train this dog. She'll never work, so don't worry about screwing her up." The truth is, I always worried about the repercussions of "screwing them up," which actually made me very good as a trainer.

I've always been a motivational trainer—always putting the focus on the positive while minimizing the negative. That Briard my dad said would never work eventually became so well-trained that I ended up paying my dad to take her off his hands. Later, after Betty had done two feature films and made numerous TV appearances, my father would tell others of how I "stole" the dog from him.

During my film training career, developing dogs became my calling card. Even my father's competitors in the industry—who also employed me—considered me a "soft trainer." That meant I could work the subpar dogs and get them through their first film or television role. Eventually these more troubled dogs could work for any trainer.

Later, I carried this soft approach into my private dog training practice. My specialty quickly became fixing the problems that dogs often have, in addition to teaching them tricks. I then pass those dogs back to their owners as I did for my father years before. Now my hope is to have the same conversation with average dog owners that

I have with my own clients. My goal as a trainer isn't simply to correct any problems the dog may have, but also to convey to the owner why the method I use is appropriate. Understanding the logic behind the training is the key to everything. If you haven't identified the problem then it's nearly impossible to eradicate its existence. This is where experience is more valuable than schooling.

My hope is that reading this book will give you the skills and insight—as well as a consistent process—to fix any problem you may run into with your canine friend.

Before you jump into Chapter One, turn to page 180 and take a look at a short glossary of some dog training terms I'll be using in this book.

CHAPTER ONE

MY HISTORY WITH DOGS, DAD, AND GRANDPA

To help you understand how and why I became the trainer I am today, I want to give you a little more background.

When I started out as a professional motion picture and television dog trainer in late 1986, it represented a second beginning for me. I had just completed four years' active service in the Navy. I looked at this as a time to pursue my perceived destiny following in the footsteps of my father and grandfather. Unlike when I entered the service—at which time my grandfather owned and trained Lassie—the responsibility for training now fell upon my father.

Grandfather Rudd had died in February 1985, and my father then inherited the title of owner and trainer of TV's most famous canine. I held on to this crazy dream that I would erase a bumpy past with my father by achieving my potential as a dog trainer and work harmoniously under his tutelage. That was not to be the case.

I learned a great deal from Dad, but the experience made the work harder than it should have been. Soon the jobs I took for my father's company decreased while my work for his competitors increased.

Later this would prove beneficial as I would learn alternative methods from other great trainers like Dennis and William Grisco, and Karl and Teresa Miller, among others. William and Teresa followed in their fathers' footsteps as I did—back then, that was the only way someone ended up as a trainer in the film industry. They learned it from their family, not from any eight-week dog training course. It was passed on from generation to generation.

Born in 1963 to Robert Walter and Linda Jean Weatherwax, I grew up an only child. Being raised with no siblings in a canine-rich environment gave me a much different perspective than most children when it came to the importance of a dog. The dogs in the Weatherwax home were major economic contributors to the household and a topic of most family conversations. These occupants were far from just being pets; the dogs always ate first and were of the highest priority. This heightened my belief that there was something quite special about dogs and that imitating them might be the key to my own significance.

Even as a baby I could frequently be seen crawling around on the floor with the dogs and drinking out of their water bowl. As soon as I had teeth, I often tested them by playing tug-of-war with the dogs. It was during those early years that I taught the dogs how to fetch and pad (play with a sock or cloth).

My father benefited from this childhood activity as it's typically very useful for movie dogs to know how to play. The sudden appearance of a favorite toy can be used to bring a frightened dog back to calmness on a movie set. So beginning as a toddler, and continuing throughout my childhood and teen years, I was the guy who taught my father's dogs how to decompress and embrace play. Then Dad would train those dogs to levels few of his competitors could duplicate.

It wasn't my original goal as a child to be a dog trainer. It seemed like a turbulent existence and my mother reminded me of this as often as she could. Growing up I looked at the dogs as a tremendous responsibility—one that could never be taken lightly. A glamorous life it wasn't, but my association with Lassie led other kids in elementary school to consider me some sort of celebrity.

I was only eleven at the time Lassie went off the air in 1974 and fourteen when my father went into business for himself. During those three in-between years, my father worked for an animal supplier named Lou Schumacher doing tough jobs with untrained dogs and becoming stressed out doing it. He didn't have the luxury of preparing a dog the way he needed to in order to get optimum results on the set. He was often given a newly acquired dog with expectations that the dog be prepared for a job immediately—sometimes as soon as the very next day. This led to my father working toward becoming a dog supplier for film and TV himself, which he did in 1976. Because of this new position, we moved about twenty miles north from Van Nuys to Canyon Country (now Santa Clarita).

The creation of my father's own animal supply company, Weatherwax Trained Dogs, turned out to be quite an undertaking. In the beginning there was just a house, a lawn, and three acres of imagination.

Suddenly kennels were being built and new dogs were being acquired. By the summer of 1977, twenty kennels had been completed. Before a fence around the kennels was erected, it was my responsibility to walk all the new dogs individually in the canyon behind our home. My mom and I rotated feeding the growing collection of dogs; my father seldom took part in these activities once he became his own boss. He believed his job was to just train the dogs, so their care was left to Mom and me.

During my teen years I was quite heavily involved in the development of my father's business. Looking back, I should have been spending more time hanging out with my friends. But I felt a responsibility that was implied, if not actually spoken, by my parents. Initially I didn't have many friends in the area anyway, as I was attending a military school near where I grew up in the San Fernando Valley.

From the time my father began the business until I left for boot camp in February 1983, I would typically clean kennels before going to school. I also still fed and walked the dogs much of the time. Joining the military liberated me from the unending worry about dogs being fed, groomed, and exercised. It was the first time in my life I only had to worry about myself.

My father's business grew during the years I served in the Navy, and by the time of my honorable discharge in 1987, there were a number of trainers working for Dad. That being the case, my dad didn't elevate me in the business as I had hoped (and assumed). Instead, I went right back to feeding the dogs and cleaning their kennels. While

I felt rejuvenated working with the dogs again, I didn't feel I should be doing the "grunt work" anymore. Eventually, thanks to skilled in-house trainers like Richard Calkins and Steven Ritt, I began as their assistant trainer. I even began working as a head trainer on some of my father's various jobs and on his competitors' gigs. My career as a freelance trainer began to climb. I simply went where the jobs were and many times during the years 1991–96, I had more jobs than I could possibly handle. I even worked in Austria for a year and a half assisting talented trainer Teresa Miller on *Kommissar Rex.*

I gained valuable experience working with great trainers like Karl Miller and Boone Narr, giving me new options in my dog training methods. I learned from every trainer I ever worked with during my time in the film industry and adopted the best techniques from each one. There were just so many talented dog trainers back then and each one offered something unique. It was the heyday of movie dog training.

Then, during the latter half of the 1990s, the industry started to change and it became harder to stay employed as a flood of young trainers entered the business—most without the responsibility of raising a family and thus willing to work for less money. The movie roles for dogs seemed to decrease as fast as the roster of trainers needing work grew.

When I came back from the job in Vienna in 1997, it was like starting over. The suppliers I used to work for had started using new trainers in my absence and by then they had achieved seniority over me. This led to me taking on other regular jobs as well as embarking on private training to supplement the sporadic movie work I was getting. I even found myself wrangling insects and livestock for film, even though this wasn't really my forte.

The day I found myself wrangling chickens for a William Hurt movie was the day I decided to walk away from training dogs for Hollywood. It had become clear that I wasn't going to be involved with Lassie as Dad had taken on a dog training assistant to avoid burnout. This led to Dad's assistant working in my father's place on a Lassie project in Canada.

Eventually, it was an easy decision to sever relations with my father when Broadway Video had the option to buy the name of "Lassie" from the Weatherwax family in 2002. My father had always told me "when I die, Lassie dies." He was wrong about that; he simply eliminated the possibility of my being involved in Lassie's future.

Regardless of the outcome of my movie training career I was determined to continue training dogs, even if only for private owners rather than movie directors. During the lean times that followed, I held other jobs but was always training dogs after work, on weekends—anytime I could. I simply couldn't get it out of my system.

Even when dogs weren't on my mind and I was working in the corporate environment, people constantly asked me about dog training. It made me think back to when I was a kid and my parents' friends would ask, "So are you going to be a dog trainer like your pop and your granddad?"

Having been named Robert Weatherwax like my dad meant that there was no escaping *that* conversation. The only problem was that much of the movie and TV work I had done previously was either credited to my father or overlooked entirely. This is simply because he was the first Robert. I was born Robert Ruddell Weatherwax and my dad was Robert Walter Weatherwax. I was given the first name of my grandfather Rudd as my middle name, much like my father, who had his grandfather Walter's first name as his middle name.

When I became a member of the Screen Actors Guild (SAG) in 1989 playing a villain in *Eyes of an Angel* with John Travolta, I took the Internet Movie Database (IMDB) and Screen Actors Guild (SAG) name of R. Ruddell Weatherwax to try to distinguish myself from my dad. Obviously, I'm still left with my grandfather's name, which I consider more of a tribute than anything else. I think if Rudd had lived long enough to see me become a dog trainer, I may have seen a different and longer journey as a Hollywood trainer. I spent many summers with Rudd during the late 1960s and '70s at his ranch helping him train the current Lassie. I was his living prop and he made me feel very special being a part of Lassie's training. He even put me in two Recipe dog food commercials with him before I was ten years old (Recipe was the official dog food of the Lassie series during the syndicated years of *Lassie* from 1970–74; it was called Recipe because it was based on my grandmother's beef stew recipe). It was Rudd who planted the seed that led to me becoming a dog trainer.

So you can see that dogs have defined me from the very beginning. I didn't choose dog training, but rather feel that it chose me. I still train dogs privately as I have ever since the end of my movie dog training years. I learned to appreciate my current clientele and have always felt that this career was for a bigger purpose than training a dog for a movie that might simply go straight to video.

I often run into repeat clients wanting me to train their second or third generation of dogs, sometimes decades after training their first. It tells me I've made a difference in their lives. There are many dogs I've trained where the training was the difference between permanent membership in a family and being returned to a shelter.

I hope this brief explanation of my experience will help you understand my motivation for writing this book. Nothing makes me happier than watching a dog owner with his or her well-trained companion.

Now let's talk about how to choose the right dog for you.

CHAPTER TWO

FIRST THINGS FIRST: CHOOSING THE RIGHT DOG

Before a dog can be trained, it must, of course, be chosen. Matching your desire to own and care for a dog with the *right* dog can make a world of difference in both your happiness and your dog's happiness. If you've already acquired your new pet, this chapter will still be useful in deciding how to adapt your new dog to your lifestyle.

The art of making a good canine acquisition involves doing a little research. Keep in mind this special soul could be living with you and your family for as long as a decade or more. It isn't a decision to be taken lightly. Accordingly, you must consider a number of factors before taking that plunge. As you read the information in this chapter, I suggest you make a checklist of the things you're willing to do daily and how much time you'll have to do them. Prior planning can make all the difference in how enjoyable dog ownership is to you—and to your dog.

ENERGY RATING

The first factor to consider is the energy level of the dog you want as your companion.

Typically, I use a scale of one to ten in determining my energy rating for a dog. This simply means how much time and effort a dog will require. A dog with a low score would be considered less active (and therefore less demanding), while one with a high score would be considered very active, thus more demanding. Then you must also give yourself a score and see if the two of you have compatible scores.

Let's say you're a jogger and lead a very active lifestyle. In this case you might be very close to the top of the human scale, making you naturally more capable of handling a high-energy dog. On the other hand, if you're very sedentary or limited physically, you probably want a dog that's more docile and controllable. It all comes down to your personal preference and capabilities.

Two factors in determining a dog's energy rating are its breed and its size. If your canine choice is a "mutt," then you must determine the combination of breeds that exist in that dog—or at least a close estimate. Keep in mind that size is a critical factor when you live in a condo or apartment, making a very large dog impractical regardless of the dog's energy score.

BREEDS

Let's look at which breeds tend to be at the higher or lower end of the energy spectrum.

If your score revealed you can handle a breed at the higher end of the scale you would probably seek a dog among the working, sporting, herding, or terrier breeds. These four broad categories of dogs were bred originally to accomplish a specific mission for his or her master and thus their natural drive typically puts them near ten on the scale.

Among the working dogs are the German Shepherds, Rottweilers, Dobermans, Mastiffs, and Huskies. Their mission was to find, protect, or serve man. Among the sporting breeds are the Pointers, Setters,

Retrievers, and Hounds. Their purpose was to either find or recover the prey of man. Then there are the herding breeds which include Collies, Border Collies, Australian Cattle Dogs, and Australian Shepherds, as well as various types of Sheepdogs. The term "herding dog" refers to those breeds specifically created to herd different types of livestock.

Finally, among the working dogs are the Terriers. These can be among the most tenacious of all breed groups since their goal was not merely to find, recover, or herd animals but to destroy them—mostly small rodents.

The aforementioned breeds represent the dogs that typically need more space to live. They need more play. They need more frequent walking. If this is something you can provide, then you're probably choosing the right dog. It's not enough to have a big backyard—but it doesn't hurt. Never confuse a walk with simply walking around the backyard. To the dog, there's just no comparison. Nothing is more wonderful to a dog than exploring the neighborhood. For them, every sniff is like getting a letter in the mail. A life without frequent walks isn't good for working *or* nonworking dogs.

It's fairly easy to determine which are the nonworking breeds. They're simply all those breeds not previously mentioned. These are dogs who were not put on this earth for a specific purpose other than to please their human companion. Poodles, Shitzus, Maltese, and other nonworking dogs fall into this category.

It's no coincidence that most of these breeds are smaller dogs; they're easily portable, giving an owner the option of carrying the dog. Size, too, is an important consideration in making your choice. Will a large dog have the space it needs to be happy?

Keep in mind there are exceptions to the rule regarding how breeds rate on my one-to-ten energy scale. This rating system is simply designed to give you an expectation of the general disposition of a particular breed. However, you may run into a typically feisty Jack Russell Terrier who isn't wired to the hilt like most of their breed . . . but it's unlikely. You might find a typically laid-back older dog that has the energy of a puppy, but that too is unlikely. These are simply trends based on my experience training well over one hundred different breeds. If you're selecting a mixed-breed dog of unknown pedigree from an animal shelter, a simple eye test is your best bet. How is the dog acting? Is he bouncing off the walls or sleeping in the corner? (For a more complete listing of dog breeds and how they rate on my energy scale, see page 183.)

OLDER VERSUS YOUNGER DOGS

In addition to breed and size, another consideration is age. Older dogs can be a great fit when you want a specific high-energy breed but don't want the juvenile version of that dog. Typically, older dogs tend to require less exercise overall. Acquiring a more mature dog also means you'll most likely be acquiring a dog that truly needs a home, whether it's from a shelter or from an owner no longer able to keep their dog. The downside is that an older dog may involve more medical costs, especially in purebred dogs.

My family has always preferred mutts. We've found it interesting to discover quite unusual mixed-breed dogs at the shelters, and the financial investment is typically less, too. Plus, getting a dog from the animal shelter saves a life that already exists.

Since my family supplied dogs to the entertainment industry, we almost always found our stars at the local pound, though Lassie was an exception. Purebreds are the dogs viewers see with the most frequency in movies and there's a good reason for that—they're easy to "double" when necessary. Many mutts are truly unique looking, making finding a suitable stunt double problematic. Choosing a mutt has the advantage of owning a one-of-a-kind dog.

RESCUE DOGS

Admirably, many people want a rescue dog to save the life of an animal that might be put to death. Keep in mind that a rescue dog will come with problems you had no part in creating. Their formative years likely came during an extended transition. There probably was nothing consistent for this dog in flux. Meals came sporadically; walks even less, if at all. Then there was the emotional aspect of living in a dysfunctional household or being re-homed at least once.

These dogs never knew structure, or if they did it was constantly interrupted. This lack of structure leads to the problems many dogs end up displaying. These are the dogs that are anxious or destructive. They're dogs desperately looking for attention. I always say that, to a dog, even bad attention is better than none. If you adopt a rescue dog or one from a shelter, are you able to cope with that dog's history and the current problems you may have to tackle—problems that aren't present with most puppies?

If your goal is to acquire a "rescue" dog, finding a local shelter is a great option as all sizes of dog—purebred and mixed—can be found there for a reasonable sum of money. The standards of care at the typical larger city shelter are above average but an online search can give you a numerical rating. There are other independent shelter options as well. In fact, the ASPCA is a good place to begin your search for a quality shelter. They normally publish a list of recommended shelters on their website, based on your location. In these days of heightened awareness on humane treatment, settle for nothing short of a "No Kill" shelter. You can also ask friends, groomers, and your local veterinarian for advice.

Growing up, my family always found our future movie dogs at one of two LA County animal shelters. We didn't have the Internet then so we had to do the "eye test" in making our choice initially. We went to the facility and checked out the cleanliness and the condition of the dogs being housed. We asked questions about the dogs we were interested in. You want to gather as much information as possible regarding the emotional and medical background of the dog. There are no stupid questions when acquiring a shelter dog.

Then, once we found success acquiring dogs from a particular shelter, we saw no reason to experiment with other facilities unless a superior one emerged by chance. It's extremely important to do your due diligence before settling on a source for your pets. It isn't a decision rooted in emotion. Even the most loving families accidentally end up with sick, aggressive, or even dying dogs all because they didn't know how to identify a good shelter.

Go to a shelter with something specific in mind—I mean specific in the way of personality, not looks. Typically, the dogs that are more relaxed—yet not at the back of the kennel—tend to be the dogs with the least issues. Even a dog that jumps up and down to meet you could be a very good dog, but might require more training than the more mellow dog. The dogs that are pacing or anxious may have some personality issues that need attention. The dog that's hiding could be shy, sick, or aggressive. You want to look for that "magic" to occur; that connection. You'll know. Sometimes a dog that may be shy with one potential owner is outgoing with another. You want to look for a connection and an energy level that seems manageable, based on your own personal standards. It's a relationship. Don't base it on what you want the dog to be but rather what he or she is now.

ACQUIRING FROM A BREEDER

You might be tempted to seek a breeder in acquiring your new best friend. Perhaps you have sentimental reasons for wanting a quality purebred. Maybe the type of dog you seek can't be found at a local shelter.

Finding a good breeder is often even more challenging than finding a quality shelter. The biggest reason is simply that shelters contain mostly older dogs whose emotional or physical shortcomings are already clearly evident. When you're buying a puppy privately there may be health or behavioral issues that don't surface until they become adults.

A reputable breeder could also be referred to as a "hobby breeder." This means they don't breed puppies for a profit, but rather for the betterment of the breed, the love of dogs, or simply for the fun of it. Since these breeders are investing more in the welfare of their dogs they will normally charge more for the puppies. You should be very wary of breeders who sell their dogs too cheaply. The term "backyard breeder" typically refers to those breeders who sell low in order to unload the puppies as quickly as possible. The sooner they unload the pups, the better their profit margin. Keep in mind that for developmental reasons puppies should not even be made available for purchase until they are at least eight to ten weeks old.

Since the inhabitants of any shelter or breeder all need homes, the hardest task will be in settling on just one dog, assuming that's your immediate goal. If your ambition is to acquire a pair (to provide a built-in playmate), I suggest mixing dogs of opposite sexes, especially if the dogs are already adults. Opposite sex blending will give you a higher probability of the two getting along well from the start and for years to come. If the two dogs in question are either littermates or puppies, same sex pairings become much easier due to either previous familiarity or overall adaptability. Adult shelter dogs often have a checkered or unknown past, making same-sex pairings potentially problematic. These older dogs are also more set in their ways, making behavior modification more challenging.

Avoid searching for any breed—mutt or purebred—on web pages like Craigslist that don't specialize in dogs. It's one thing to search there for a nonliving entity, like a computer, but not one that requires proper care and feeding. There are just too many so-called "breeders" out there who are simply out to reap their "puppy harvest" while investing the least in their actual breeding and handling. These are the places often referred to as "puppy mills" or the aforementioned "backyard breeders." There are no standards of care in these places and limited accountability if you get a physically or emotionally damaged dog. Risking redundancy, dogs in these places are raised in quantity for profit; not in fewer numbers where overall quality is easier to achieve.

These makeshift facilities are often poorly maintained and overcrowded. There isn't a great deal of human interaction for the dogs—which is important for developing canine minds. These breeders often have little experience and didn't begin the line with stellar ingredients.

Many a genetic line of dog begins with a dog that has some sort of defect, like hip dysplasia or epilepsy. You may not be aware of it at the time you first acquire the offspring of such a dog, but the long-term implications will be more difficult to overlook. This is why visiting the site of the breeder is recommended no matter what reputation precedes them. The eye test is certainly a must. Have you seen the parents? If you're not able to witness the health of the "line," you should be wary.

Ask your veterinarian if they know of a reputable breeder in your area or ask close friends who own healthy dogs of the same breed as your target dog. You can also contact local breed clubs or visit professional dog shows and strike up a conversation with participants or spectators to see if they know of a good breeder.

You can also find out if a breeder is in good standing with the AKC (American Kennel Club) by contacting AKC customer service at (919) 233-9767 or info@akc.org. Whether it's at a kennel or at the breeder's home, a face-to-face meeting is a must. Don't rely on the phone. Go in person.

As mentioned, the best time to acquire a puppy from a breeder or elsewhere is somewhere around ten weeks of age. I've run into many clients who acquired puppies prior to the tender age of eight weeks only to find that these puppies seem to have more socialization defects than dogs that stayed with their mother and siblings a bit longer.

MALE OR FEMALE

As to your new dog's gender, males and females tend to have very different dispositions—again with exceptions, of course. My experience is that male dogs tend to be a bit more active than females, and also more outgoing.

My father was so convinced of the male dog's outgoing nature that he didn't choose to train female dogs after going into business for himself. He simply felt that a male would be a bit more emotionally stable than a female. Though there may be some truth to that, I've loved working with female dogs. They can be a bit more sensitive. I know my grandfather Rudd considered them better learners than male dogs but like my dad, felt they were less resilient.

It was me who ended up training Dad's female dogs. I was so good at building up dogs that I normally was given the less confident dogs, not only on Dad's jobs but also his competitors' jobs. That was my specialty. If there was a dog that was a little shaky, I ended up working with them and breaking them in for other trainers to work later. I always took more pride in elevating the underdog to perform than training the naturally good dog to perform. It could be more challenging but it made training success with them all the more rewarding.

My female Briard, Betty, from *Dennis the Menace* and *Top Dog* was much like my dog Prince when I started with her. A few years later she was among the best trained of her breed in the industry and ended up working more than many of my dad's male dogs. Along with Buck from *Married with Children,* she put this then-rare breed on the map.

I may have spent some extra time with exposure and confidence as I trained Betty, but it was the best investment I ever made. She ended up becoming tolerant to everything and as a result became more resilient. She was always very trainable but without the exposure she would never have endured the chaos of a movie set.

The one thing that never changed with Betty was her softness. While she became a very brave and tolerant dog, my voice tone was always a bit elevated with her. Since she lacked natural energy, it was my voice that got her going. I never said "no" to Betty. It just wasn't necessary. Offering praise or omitting praise were my only training options. Betty never gave me cause to reprimand her since any harsh tone made her crumble emotionally. That was the last thing you'd want to happen on a movie set.

Speaking of a dog's emotions, please know that dogs, like humans, *do* have emotions! In fact, most of their emotions are mirror images of their owners. If their owner gets upset in certain situations, the dog will pick that up and show similar anxiety, even in the absence of the owner who created it. Dogs are also very sensitive to vibrations and can detect changes in the heartbeat and breathing of the people around them. When a dog senses fear it has a distinct smell that often resembles aggression.

DOGS AND CHILDREN

I'm often asked what the best breed of dog is for children. This is difficult to answer because I believe in the individuality of all dogs, regardless of breed. However, as a general rule, Retrievers tend to be the most reliable choice as they are typically the most tolerant and gentle of all breeds.

While Goldens and Labs are generally considered hunting breeds there are many herding breeds that are great with kids, as they're natural guardians. Breeds like Collies, Border Collies, and Briards can be good choices. In general, the female gender works better with kids as they tend to be less excitable than their male counterparts. Again, this is just a general rule and there are always exceptions.

By the way, speaking of kids, I feel that allowing the kids to have a specific role in training will keep them from becoming too much of a distraction. Kids can get jealous of the attention given to the dog, so we want to keep everyone in the loop so that young egos aren't damaged and no jealousy is created.

I'm also frequently asked which breed is my personal favorite. My favorite small breed is the Beagle, as I had one as a kid. They are also a great choice for a family with children. My favorite larger breed is probably the Collie for obvious reasons. I like both the Rough and Smooth versions of the breed.

GROOMING

Another consideration when choosing a dog has to do with grooming. Are you willing to put in the time and money to keep a long-haired dog adequately groomed? I often see owners with very exotic long-haired dogs whose coat is a complete disaster. They're either matted or simply shaved out of necessity. The owners didn't take grooming or maintenance into account when they chose their dog. Grooming requirements will play a big part in the basic needs of your dog.

Betty, my Briard French Sheepdog was quite a challenge to keep well-groomed. I had the energy then to brush her constantly, but I'm not sure I'd want to spend that much time doing it now. It's a lot of work. The good news is that during the summer you can give your dog a summer cut. I didn't have that luxury with Betty as she landed movie work due to her distinct shaggy look.

PERSONALITY IS IMPORTANT

One additional factor in choosing your dog is being aware of each dog's personality. Just like people, every dog has a unique personality—meaning each dog often requires a different approach. Even puppies from the same litter will have completely unique personalities. These factors are all relevant with people as well—my two daughters, Jean and Brooke, resemble opposite sides of the same coin. They're different based on their life experiences as well as the fact they have a twelve-year age difference—and were parented differently as a result. Jean ended up becoming a police officer and Brooke a registered nurse. Most importantly, they are individuals and I love each for their own authenticity.

You'll find that life with your new canine pal is going to be a lot about building their self-esteem. A dog with a confident personality will always be more responsive to your commands, making you more confident in issuing them.

I can't count the number of times I've seen dog owners hassling their dogs over things that don't matter: things like eating a little grass, occasionally exploring beyond their assigned boundaries, or some other benign act. Dogs need to figure things out on their own—to some degree. They never will when there's a figurative stop sign everywhere they look. You will want to save the corrections for acts that are either dangerous or truly aggravating to you.

It's hard for me to even imagine my life without a dog. I've been around dogs nearly my entire life. I consider them to be a great responsibility, but one worth taking on. The joy given me by the thousands of dogs I've known has far exceeded my efforts in training and caring for them. Dogs are the yardstick in my world. They look upon me as someone greater than I could ever be. They give me far more than I've ever given them—and I've given them virtually my entire life.

Between my film and private training career I've worked with virtually every existing breed of dog, plus a multitude of mutts. I've worked with large and small dogs, male and female, ornery and sweet-tempered. The majority of dogs weren't movie dogs hoping to get a job, these were dogs who merely wanted a home. Since each dog is an individual—based on background and breed—I don't even begin to envision a training approach until I know what behavioral flaws the dog is displaying upon my first view.

Many of these dogs didn't need training as much as they needed consistency in their lives. They needed to know that the home they left would be the same home they had upon their arrival. Since dogs absolutely crave structure, keeping their schedule as consistent as possible always leads to a happier dog. Even when your own schedule is running amok, will you be able to minimize wholesale change in their life?

OTHER CONSIDERATIONS

In addition to the nature of the dog itself, there are other considerations. Will you have the dog spayed or neutered? Obviously, if you're going to breed your dog, the answer would be no. But in other cases, the best answer is yes. Vets may disagree with me and breeders have their own idea of the perfect time for their personal chosen breed. I believe ten months is normally the optimal time for getting your dog fixed, females even a little sooner. My fifty-five years of experience also lead me to believe waiting a bit longer allows for more complete development, hormonally, especially in males. Getting dogs fixed is not only a health benefit but also can deter aggression in both males and females.

You'll also want to select a good veterinarian. Ask friends for recommendations.

Additionally, you'll need to decide if you should buy insurance for your dog. The answer is yes, especially if you have a purebred. Mutts, due to their broad gene pool, simply have fewer maladies than pedigree dogs. My clients have told me many tales of how their pet insurance saved them thousands of dollars within the first two years. It's a cost worth paying, but obviously cheaper to own with a younger dog.

As you can see, there are many factors to consider before getting a dog. It's not a decision that can be made in a single day. You need to have all your ducks in a row before making this important decision. You should have a routine in mind for your dog before he or she arrives. You should also think about safety in the home. Just like raising children, you must dog-proof your home. Make sure you've already discovered any potential hazards with the dog and know the solution before facing them.

CHECK YOUR MOTIVATION

Before you make that final choice, make sure of your motive for acquiring a dog. If your intention is to simply have a dog, then you really shouldn't have one at all.

Owning a dog isn't like buying a suit. Dogs aren't accessories. They can be so understanding when no one else understands. They never argue or lie to you. They can be more trustworthy than anyone you've known. The only way you make a friend like this is to invest in the relationship wholeheartedly. Anything worth doing is worth doing well. You must choose wisely.

Take your time making that big decision. Don't rush in and simply acquire a dog out of emotion. My extensive experience with dog training tells me one theme above all: Whether you acquire a purebred or a mutt, or you visit a shelter or a breeder, the happiest dog owners are the most informed ones. The extra time you spend doing research will turn a cloudy future to one with clarity.

CHAPTER THREE

DAY ONE: INTRODUCING A NEW MEMBER TO THE HOUSEHOLD

The day you bring your dog home is a happy day for both you and your new best friend. There are some basic principles that will make homecoming easier and will set the tone for a happy future. I think the principle that best sums it up is one I learned in the Navy. It was the five P's: Prior Planning Prevents Piss-Poor Performance.

You will need to plan ahead to make sure the new resident has a place to sleep, food and water, and is ready to be trained from day one.

Yes, training begins on this very first day. The new member of the household needs to learn what they can and cannot do starting the day they arrive. This requires teaching them the location of their bathroom and showing them their bed. They will immediately learn where they will eat and where water (always available) can be found.

I recommend having a "puppy pen," dog crate, or some other enclosed area as their feeding place, unless you're feeding the dog outside. The point of feeding them in a puppy pen or an enclosed area is so they have the option of relieving themselves immediately if you're not able to take them out. Remember, the younger the puppy, the less control they have of their bladder.

Typically, a puppy pen is four-sided, forming a vertical square that can be moved from place to place. The idea is to have a restroom in the house as well as out. This way the facilities are never far away. This just makes getting him or her to their pee place an easier process for you, the trainer.

It's safe to say that soon after—if not immediately upon—arriving home they'll want to go to the bathroom. Therefore the very first place they should go after walking through the door will be outside. Be specific; if you want them to go in a particular place then you go to that place and tell them to pee—one time. Don't say it over and over as it will distract them from the task at hand. If they resist going where you want them to go, put on your long leash and don't give them enough leash to leave that area. Ignore them until they go, at which time you would make a big fuss with praising them, acting like it's the best thing they've ever done. That act of going where you want them to go is what earns them the right to be in the house or loose outside of their appointed alternative bathroom area.

The question then becomes how often they should go. The answer is pretty obvious with adult dogs—after meals and drinking or after

increased activity. Puppies are a completely different story; it's almost like carrying a pitcher and trying not to spill it. It seems that every time you put a puppy down in your house, they want to go. Assuming you're feeding your young puppy three times a day, you can expect them to need to go immediately after each of those meals. I do mean *immediately*. This also applies to anytime they drink water. I also recommend you feed them in either their puppy pen or the backyard as this will make them feel positive about these places. Then if they have to go, they're already in the right place.

In fact, I would keep the puppy pen open when the puppy isn't being confined so if you aren't tuned in, they have the option of going there as a personal choice. If they make the right choice they should know it was the right choice. You should also place the water and toys in one or both of these containment areas. These are not to be considered bad places, but locations where a certain goal—relieving themselves—is to be accomplished. I line the bottom of the indoor pen with newspapers or puppy pads so the dog recognizes they're going on a surface different than your linoleum or carpeting. Dogs young and old begin to make that distinction right away. You just have to be consistent.

If the dog goes in either the puppy pen or yard, they're rewarded with freedom. If they have an accident in the wrong place, they must be confined to either the indoor or outdoor enclosure until they go. There is no punishment involved. I would just say something like "Lassie, this is not good, let me take you over here," and then put them in their pen or yard and wait. It's all said firmly, but matter-of-factly.

If they go again—which is what we hope—then they're free again. If they don't go, then they have to stay there or be relocated to their other approved pee spot. If they just stand there and won't go, just take a step away from them while ignoring them. The mere need to move often gets them to go. The bottom line is they must earn freedom.

You might be asking, "If not after meals or drinking, what's a good indication my pup may want to go?" The best indication is when they begin sniffing around (at nothing), followed by a circular spin. You should be already on your way to get them when they sniff too long. You would immediately take them to either containment area and wait for them to go. Then freedom will reign once again. Be suspicious of the puppy going to rooms in the house that are empty. Closing bedroom and bathroom doors will force them to be closer to you. Soon they'll begin to give you a signal when they want to go. It could be a whine or signal saying, "I'm uncomfortable" or by actually going to their pen or to the door leading to the backyard. Since not everyone has a doggy door in their house, I've encouraged many of my clients to hang a bell by the door at the dog's level for ringing. Just make sure when that bell rings that you're there to answer.

While developing the bathroom routine for your dog it's vital that it blends well with your routine. There's no need to change your life-style for your dog; consider your dog an enhancement. If you're fully invested in raising your puppy right, then there are no alternatives to doing it the right way from the very beginning.

FEEDING

If your new friend is a puppy, it will need to eat three or four times a day to start, removing the food bowl after fifteen or so minutes. Never "free-feed," meaning don't leave the food for them to nibble all day. Keep the bowl on the floor for fifteen minutes or until the dog finishes; whichever comes first. Dogs—especially the smaller breeds—will develop poor eating habits when their food is always available. They'll always choose something with an expiration date over something that is infinite. This creates an urgency to eat—which is a healthy trait. After the age of six months—or if your new dog is an adult—feeding times can be twice a day for the rest of their lives.

The foundation of a meal for dogs, young and old, is some type of dry food. This is good for the dog's teeth and provides most of the nutritional value in the canine meal. However, feeding it dry isn't too tantalizing to most dogs. As a result, I recommend adding a bit of warm water and let the kibble sit in it for about five minutes. We don't want it to end up mushy; just crunchy in the middle.

Beyond that, you can add a small amount of canned food for flavor, but be creative in this area. If you'd like to add meat or vegetables to a dog's meal, it would be a healthy alternative to canned food. I would stay away from pork as it is hard for dogs to digest. Any other meat would be acceptable as long as you are sure there are no bones remaining; even boneless fish would work. The vegetables you add are best steamed.

ENTERING THE HOUSE

Before you enter the house, it's a good idea to give your new dog a thorough walk outside to give it a chance to relieve itself. Dogs are always capable of wanting to mark a new place; even if there are no other animal smells present. If they don't have a full bladder, they will be much less likely to mark your home.

Upon entering the house, the new dog should be allowed to investigate the entire living space. We want to discover—as soon as possible—if there's anything the dog wants to chew or any place they want to mark. We won't correct the dog for simply checking out things. Our goal is to discover what might be an issue later. The less interference you offer, the better idea you'll have of their natural behavioral tendencies. When you interrupt a dog's bad behavior before they are fully invested in it, you're only teaching them to better conceal their unfavorable behavior.

Their routine from the first day should change as little as possible. Whatever rules are put in place when they arrive are the rules they should adhere to a year or five down the road. If they're tempted to jump on furniture, then that tendency should be curtailed right away. Good behavior should be expected early and often. The definition of good behavior is whatever you make it.

Your first impulse may be to play with the new member, but play time can better be focused on after the rules are clear. There's no need to be strict; just consistent. You're not being cruel to your dog by correcting them for making mistakes. If you don't let them slide on the rules, there will be no bad habits to break later on. The mere tolerance of bad behavior represents approval to the dog. The longer the bad behavior is tolerated, the harder it will be to correct it later on.

The leash the dog wears to get in and out of your car should remain on the dog until he or she has fully looked over his or her new

living space. It will also be much more convenient correcting any immediate bad behavior if the dog is already wearing a leash.

Only when your new friend becomes bored with their surroundings will you remove the leash. There's almost always some degree of apprehension or excitement when a dog first enters any home, depending on the disposition of the dog. Whether your dog is "wild" or "shy," they will find calmness and/or security knowing your expectations right away. They will also naturally behave better with a leash on than off.

All the family members should be familiar with the rules you set for the dog. The rules required by one family member should be followed by all. If one family member is letting the dog break the rules, the dog's behavior will suffer, affecting everyone in the family.

Visitors can often cultivate bad behavior. Extended family members can often be the greatest distraction. They often welcome jumping and barking. Try to avoid allowing any visitors to contradict calm behavior by your dog through overstimulation. This can appear in the form of baby talk or giving the dog too much attention upon arrival. You also don't want your dog to initiate physical contact with any visitor who isn't comfortable with it. I never initiate petting any dog I meet unless they have first sniffed me all over. I often endure the sniffing process with my arms folded so the movement of my hands doesn't become an issue.

CRATE TRAINING

Teaching your dog to accept temporary confinement is very important. Teaching that lesson early means the dog won't rebel against it later. The process of confinement doesn't mean simply throwing them into a kennel or crate without a gradual introduction.

When acquiring a mini dog kennel or crate for your dog, there are a couple of things that are important. First, it must be large enough for the dog: they should be able to enter and turn inside without difficulty. Second, the dog should not be locked in their new enclosure initially. The key is to allow them to become comfortable there first with the door open.

Creating a positive connotation of the crate for your dog is job number one. Everything that's important for your dog should originate there. They should be fed there, have water either inside or nearby, and their toys should originate there. I even would go as far as to periodically plant treats there when the dog isn't looking so they begin to believe that food grows there.

When your dog begins to feel comfortable being enclosed we can begin closing the kennel door while they're inside. This prepares them for the times when they may be alone in the house. Often a bored dog alone can be destructive. I would suggest the door be closed first while they're eating since they will be distracted. It's important not to engage in a great deal of eye contact while the dog is enclosed and refrain from talking to them. Looking or talking to your dog will serve as a tease for your dog since it will make them focus more on being separated from the household. We want to act as if it's no big deal, and go about our business. Occasionally you may drop a goody into the crate but only while the dog is calm.

In the beginning, locking your dog up may seem cruel especially when you're home and it's not necessary. However, if done regularly, for no reason, the dog will begin to look at it as routine. If you wait until you actually leave them alone, it will only signify abandonment. The crate shouldn't have any specific connotation at all; which is why we must make them comfortable inside before they're left alone.

A dog that's crated early and often will begin to find security there. It will begin to be common for your dog to choose to sleep there, even if they're not eating, drinking, or going for a toy. Once again, dogs love structure and leaving a dog alone in an empty apartment or house is an uncertain proposition. The dog is thinking, *what am I supposed to do now?* This is the thought they have just before they begin destroying the furniture or other household items. Eventually the dog will enjoy the crate so much you'll be able to leave the door open even when you leave. They believe that simply by residing in the crate you will return, since you always have during their training.

It's important to continue providing all their necessities from inside the crate. If I were a dog, why would I want to be in a crate if I receive my food and water in the kitchen? Why would I stay there if my toys are outside of my crate? Why would I go to the bathroom in the crate if I get away with peeing anywhere? The crate will become the center of their universe and your dog will gravitate toward it; as long as you don't turn it into something negative or meaningless.

Remember that dogs revolve around patterns and labels. Once a dog gets used to the pattern, then they give it a label in their own mind. Dogs only see things in two ways: right or wrong. Maybe or sometimes mean nothing to a dog. Keep in mind that if your dog suffers from Separation Anxiety (see Chapter Nine) *and* lacks housebreaking skills, a layer of newspaper lining the bottom of the crate will give you additional peace of mind.

Just to be clear, the crate is not a place of punishment, it's more simply a temporary loss of freedom. There's no anger or punishment associated with it. When they're put in their crate, they already have everything they need inside.

The punishment is in losing their freedom. That is all. While it may seem like the punishment doesn't always fit the crime; guess again. Remember that the worst punishment you can ever give your dog—or your child—is to simply ignore them.

When your dog starts feeling more comfortable inside the crate it will begin to represent a safe haven wherever you go. When I worked in the film industry, all my dogs had to learn to travel in a crate since I often had to transport more than one dog. In the absence of a canine seat harness, a mini-kennel represents the safest mode of transporting canines.

When clients don't see the value of crate-training, I like to tell them the tragic story about two Hollywood animal trainers who were traveling on a two-lane highway in Santa Clarita here in the Los Angeles area. In the back of their Ford Econoline van, they had six dogs in plastic pet carriers (what we called crates) while they themselves wore the antiquated lap belts. They ended up getting into a head-on collision with another car and, with no air bags in that era, both human occupants were killed by their lap belts. One of the dogs in the back suffered a broken leg, but the other dogs weren't physically injured in any way. What would have happened if those dogs were loose in the car? What's more cruel? A few hours of confinement or intentionally putting your dog into the barrel of the cannon?

Telling this story tends to elevate overall enthusiasm for crate training. It's even more important while traveling to make sure the crate isn't too big—for safety purposes. This will keep the dog from injuring themselves when flying from one end of the crate to the other in a similar accident. It will protect them better by being a bit smaller. Many clients end up utilizing two separate crates: a large one for the house and a smaller one for traveling. Remember to always feed the dog upon entering the crate, even after their fear of it has subsided. Training isn't just about learning; it's about maintenance.

Hopefully, you'll begin to recognize the importance of crate training, even if you never actually have to use one. It's a great fallback plan for any dog. It can bring a lot of comfort to a dog that's being evacuated or in another situation where you're forced to leave under duress. It's also a great way to give a dog a routine time-out for poor behavior. That time-out will make a point but will have no negative connotation to the dog other than relinquishing their freedom, albeit temporarily. While a crate is most useful for the more nervous dog, it can be used to settle the outgoing dog. I can't think of anything that could justify not teaching them about measured confinement.

IF THE NEW DOG IS A SECOND DOG

One common situation many dog owners don't anticipate is how to introduce the new dog into a household as a second dog, where a previous dog is still present. Many dog lovers feel that once the effort required for your first dog has been minimized, it's now time to consider taking on another dog. The presence of a trained "veteran" dog in your household can only ease the transition for the new "rookie" canine member. Still, there are a few ways to make the transition easier.

Whether you first began your dog ownership journey with one dog or multiple dogs, the immediate priority with a second dog is to get the newbie accepted by all the current residents of the household. This process should be taken seriously as there are many potential issues that can occur. Particularly, the complexity of the first meeting can be compounded by either dog having socialization issues from the outset.

First impressions are huge as the first meeting between strangers, as with people, sets the tone for all future meetings. How much socialization have the "veteran" and "rookie" dog had prior to meeting? Each dog's personal history has a lot to do with the approach you might take. For a moment, let's assume both dogs have relatively good social skills.

The first thing to consider is that initially the resident dog has the home field advantage. He or she has had things go their way for some time. They haven't had to share with another dog. It's like an only child meeting their new sibling for the first time. There might be a little culture shock over giving up being the center of attention. We dilute that advantage by placing a training collar and leash on the resident dog prior to meeting the new dog.

The arriving dog should be equally disarmed by also wearing their own training leash and collar. They should first meet outside of the house or yard on neutral territory. Neutral territory is any place the resident dog hasn't already claimed as their possession.

A sidewalk or neighboring yard would be a good location as these places normally hold no emotional value for either dog.

Once each dog has accepted the other "on leash" and on neutral territory, the two dogs can enter the house. It's best for the visiting dog to enter first as this would deny the resident dog the opportunity to reestablish territorial superiority. All food bowls and toys should be put away prior to the dogs entering the house, at least initially. After both dogs have entered the house, the leashes can be dropped but still worn.

There will be a period where the new dog will want to check out everything in the house and often they might find something like a stray toy or a dog bed that's a trigger to the resident dog. The leashes won't be taken off until the discovery process is complete and the dogs begin taking the other for granted. Remember, it's not friendship we're trying to achieve, only acceptance. When both dogs are ignoring the other is when you know they've achieved mutual acceptance.

If there's more than one resident dog, the same rules apply, though each veteran dog would meet the new dog separately before they all enter the home. Once again, the new dog will enter first while the resident dog with the poorest social skills enters last. The leashes of all the dogs will stay on until *all* the dogs are equally bored with one another. I never use food rewards in the presence of multiple dogs unless all are proven to not be food aggressive.

Food aggressiveness is a dog's way of resource-guarding in which the dog becomes very defensive when eating, using threats to force others away. It can be directed toward other animals, humans, or both.

These threats can appear initially through growling when there is a perceived threat to what they already have or, in some cases, to what they would like to have. That growling can lead to snapping and eventually biting anyone who challenges their ownership of food or a coveted item, which can include bones and certain toys.

It's also important that no favoritism is shown to any of the dogs in clear view of the others. Once a new routine is established—one that includes the new dog—then the rules can begin to loosen and you'll discover what each dog will tolerate of the others.

What if either the resident dog or the new dog is aggressive toward the other upon meeting the first time on neutral territory? Whether it's the new dog exhibiting fear/aggression or the resident dog, the offending dog must be kept about ten to fifteen feet away from the calm dog until the aggressive behavior dissipates. Over time both dogs will become bored and lie down. This would be our cue to once again initiate one-on-one meetings. The bottom line is we must have two dogs that have grown indifferent toward each before entering the personal domain of *either* dog.

My experience has shown me that it's normally the resident dog that has more anxiety on the initial meeting. This is why I can't stress enough the importance of letting the resident dog watch the visiting dog enter their home before entering themselves. Any problem that might emerge will be evident at the moment the resident dog sees the visiting dog enter "their" home. Are they showing anxiety or are they sniffing a bush? These signals tell you a lot about who is the dog that must be supervised more closely. Friendship will develop over time between the dogs; too much roughhousing in the beginning can lead to problems.

Often one dog is naturally more sociable than the other dog. That more social dog must not be allowed to overwhelm the dog not as eager to meet.

Look for signs of a dog not as eager to play or be jumped on. This dog may eventually become aggressive if pushed beyond their own comfort level. This interaction must be monitored, making sure each dog is comfortable with the level of contact. Only when both dogs are comfortable can the leashes be removed.

Introducing a new canine family member isn't a lot different than meeting dogs on the street, except in the latter situation both dogs are normally already on neutral territory. There is no home field advantage. When I'm walking clients' dogs and socializing them on the street, I'm wary of any approaching dog that's *too* anxious to meet mine. I'll also bring in the reins on the dog I'm training if he or she is pulling hard to meet the other dog. Both dogs should be calm before they're allowed to meet. Slow the dogs down prior to meeting as they tend to speed up again naturally once they get comfortable with one another. By the same token, rushing a meeting that both dogs aren't ready for can create problems. Don't rush the one-on-one encounter; let it happen casually and be patient.

A CAT IN THE HOUSE

What if you're adding another animal to the family like a cat or bird? Is the process different? This addition could seem like a non-event to many dog owners. However, there are some adopted dogs that have never actually seen anything other than dogs well into their lives. Now, at two years of age, they're seeing a cat for the first time. Some dogs might consider this the equivalent to you witnessing an alien spacecraft landing on your lawn.

Putting yourself in your dog's shoes allows you to view their aggressive or timid behavior as justifiable. The more familiar a dog becomes with the new animal's movement, the better. The new animal will also need to observe the behavior of the resident dog in order to feel comfortable around him or her. Once again, the responsibility of harmony falls upon the resident dog.

When a new cat enters the home they should not be carried by hand. This will give the impression that you're holding "live bait," often causing an anxious dog to try pulling that object down to the ground. Since the dog will be on a leash and training collar, you'll be able to control the dog at all times.

The cat should be brought into the house in a carrier. The cat in the carrier will simply be placed on the floor in the same room as the dog, initially by someone not holding the dog. Then the process of desensitization will begin. Only when the dog is fully aware of the "cat in the box" and no longer cares, should you consider opening the carrier door, freeing the cat. Chances are the cat will be just as surprised at seeing the dog as the dog will be seeing the cat.

Some cats will just run and hide upon leaving their carrier. This behavior will probably lead the dog to searching for the cat. It's fine to let him look for the cat, but on leash where the dog can be controlled, should the cat emerge from their hiding place. Plan to pay the dog a food reward periodically for calm behavior whether the cat is in the carrier or free in the house. Always let the dog observe the cat when supervised. Anytime the dog is in the same room as a free cat, that dog must be on a leash and training collar and continually rewarded for good behavior. The cat will never be restrained, but a distraction tool may be used on the cat if he or she becomes too forward with the dog.

Once again, mutual acceptance is a must. Any contract must include two willing parties. Passive behavior starts the relationship in the right place. Then good behavior will drive the relationship forward, evolving naturally. Nothing is forced and each animal must respect the other, even if they don't exhibit love for one another.

As time goes by, the cat will leave the dog alone while also becoming comfortable in their own right. The dog will begin to see the futility in pursuing the cat. You can then consider taking the leash off while leaving the collar on, initially. That decision will be executed when not only the dog and the cat are comfortable, but you are as well.

After the leash is off, a distraction tool can still be used on either the dog or cat if unacceptable behavior reemerges from one or both (for an explanation of a distraction tool, see page 44). A distraction tool can be a concealed thrown object or something like a stomp on the ground, or a clap of the hands (but no yelling). A distraction should never be generated from your mouth. It exhibits a lack of control on your part that the dog will easily recognize and use against you. The most effective distraction tool is a chain collar if the training collar you're using is also a chain collar, though there might be a time when using a chain collar is not an available option. Whatever distraction you use, make sure a reward is offered afterwards, assuming the bad behavior has waned.

Once all the nonhuman family members are cohabiting peacefully, the first meal will present itself as the next pivotal moment in the new dog's or cat's first day. I've always fed cats separately from dogs, no matter how well they seem to get along. I wouldn't even feed them in the same room as the dogs. This is kind of the natural order of things; dogs here, cats there.

Now that we've moved past the cat question at mealtime, let's focus on how the feeding will transpire between the canine co-residents. Since the resident dog or dogs already have an established routine and feeding order, you won't change that. You'll simply add the new dog's feeding to the end of that routine in a separate area at first.

If there is a food possessive dog in the group, you'll feed that dog in another room, much like we did with the cat. The new dog will receive their food last. We don't want to disrupt the accepted order of things unless absolutely necessary. I've always believed that dogs should eat in separate rooms as a general rule. I'm not saying there aren't exceptions, but mealtime cooperation between multiple dogs should never be assumed.

Whether you choose to feed the dogs in one room or separate ones, a reminder that you should never free-feed, leaving bowls with food lying around long after the meal is first offered. This not only creates picky eaters, since there is no urgency to finish, it also can create a random dog fight that could have easily been avoided.

There should be a maximum time given—normally ten to fifteen minutes—for all the dogs to eat before the bowls are removed. The slowest-eating dog's food can often become a target for the dog or dogs that have already finished. If this type of glutinous behavior can't be curtailed, then the slowest-eating dog should be fed in a separate room until their time is up.

While you can easily create time limits for the dogs to finish their food, it's not in the nature of most other animals to eat in a certain time frame. It's not really an issue with the bird, fish, lizard, hamster, etc., since they normally eat in an aquarium or cage. They can safely eat in their enclosure. These enclosures are normally too high for the dog to reach so these other pets aren't an issue.

Cats, on the other hand, tend to eat the slowest of all domestic pets. They also spend a lot of their time on dressers and other elevated furniture locations around the house. For this reason, I would permit them to free-feed. You just want to make sure that like your other smaller pets, their food bowl is kept above the reach of the comparatively earthbound dogs. I don't know why it is, but very few dogs can resist the temptation of sampling some of that horrible-smelling cat food. Whether it smells bad or not, it's considered quite an unexpected delicacy by many dogs. It could also become a bone of contention among dogs, all wanting a bite of it.

Owning multiple pets is like having multiple children. It's like a collective teeter-totter and we always must keep it in balance. If one dog perceives the other dog or pet getting better treatment, that can lead them to plot that pet's demise. It may not happen today or next week, but it will happen if equality doesn't reestablish itself.

The two biggest triggers for altercations between canine family members are food and toys. Food is an easy fix for me because I never feed one dog in the presence of another unless I'm feeding that dog as well. Toys are a little different. Certain toys will hold more meaning to a particular dog than another toy. There are various reasons this occurs but if a dog is too possessive with a particular toy, I normally trade a goody for that toy and make it disappear for a while. Dogs that are possessive over personal toys are the reason I never recommend my clients taking their dogs to dog parks. Fights often start there over the presence of a dog's personal toy. I also believe that all household toys should be stored in their toy box when not in use. This way no dog can establish their geographical kingdom around one particular toy. It also keeps the toys exciting to all the dogs. Dogs tend to value something they have to travel for over something right in front of them. They often only become possessive over something they have had too long.

When training more than one dog, it's best to train the dogs separately for all behaviors except "stay" (on a mark) and "heel." These two behaviors can eventually be done as a group, assuming all have equal skills doing it on their own.

Training of tricks like "shake" and "crawl" should always be done independently. It's just too hard to reward and correct multiple dogs simultaneously when all are at different stages of their training.

If doing "stay" or "heel" as a group, just remember that all get a food reward or none do. Typically if all the dogs are good at something there's no need for a food reward no matter what they're doing. However, if you feed just once, all must be fed once. It's all part of the balance you want in your household. We want all our dogs to feel they belong and are equal.

I have a client who has multiple young dogs but also has another elderly dog who would constantly try escaping the house. Once I added a special session for her in addition to my two-hour session with the other dogs, she no longer tried escaping. She simply wanted to feel as important as the other dogs. She didn't need training, but she needed to participate. Equal participation by all canine members will create harmony and confidence for all. This way no dog decides to take up a bad behavior just out of sheer perceived negligence.

All dogs are capable of getting along. It might be easier for some than others, but it can always be done. I'm the eternal optimist for a reason. The reason most dogs don't get along is because they were never really made to do it. They were either kept separate, treated differently from one another, or were unfixed males. There just aren't many other reasons dogs cannot live harmoniously together. Before being domesticated by man, they ran in packs and cooperated with one another. No dog operated independently. Dogs are naturally social creatures and not normally eccentric. It's our habits that often empower one dog to feel superior or inferior to the others. We must always remain aware of how our dogs are interpreting our actions as well as how we perceive theirs.

In the next chapter we'll delve into the tools you'll need to begin training your dog. There won't be pinch collars or shock collars involved. There will be no sitting on your dog or administering any punishment. The methods being taught today tend to stress discipline more than developing character. I believe that both are equally important.

CHAPTER FOUR

TOOLS OF THE TRADE (AND TOOLS I DO *NOT* RECOMMEND)

Virtually every occupation you can imagine is propelled by equipment or tools that enable a worker to do their job more efficiently. Much like a carpenter has his hammer and nails and a plumber has his pipe wrench and flashlight, a dog trainer must have the right tools in order to get the most out of their four-legged student.

A lack of confidence on your part will always impede your training, as the most important vibe a dog can feel from their owner/trainer is one of confidence without fear. This necessary confidence can come from following a simple process involving just two training tools and one "distraction" tool. Let's focus on our training tools first.

LONG LEASH, SHORT LEASH

The number-one training tool is the long lead or "training leash." It's normally made of nylon and can range in length from ten to fifty feet. I recommend starting with a fifteen-foot leash and then moving to a longer one if you first build a comfort level with the fifteen-footer—many of my students struggle with the thirty- and fifty-foot leashes I often use in my training. You will also want a second, shorter, leash for indoor training.

Using a long leash is an acquired skill and some wonder why a long leash is preferred over the shorter leash. Simply put, a longer leash allows you to develop control with your dog from a distance—the key to my training when working in the film industry. How many times did I have to be hundreds of feet away from my dog while putting them through a series of commands in movies and on TV? The answer to that question is *often*, as the presence of movie cameras always meant that being close to the dog on set was unrealistic.

Assuming your goal is to be able to eventually trust your dog "off leash" then how would you accomplish that using a four-foot-long leash? The answer is *you don't*. That would be the equivalent of going from kindergarten to college. We need something that serves as a bridge from the short leash to nothing at all. The longer training leash gives you control from a distance right off the bat. This will enable you to develop the two most important commands ("Stay" and "Come") quickly and without harsh methods.

The key to handling a long leash is to envision that it's a Cobra and you only want to focus on the head. If there's leash dragging behind you, you're probably doing it right. You start out by walking the dog on your preferred side using the command "Heel."

In handling only the top of the leash and letting the rest drag, you have extra leash to give your dog should he or she seek a private place to go to the bathroom. If I were the dog, I certainly wouldn't want my owner to be right behind me when I relieve myself. You can give the dog that extra space by simply letting the leash slide through your hands. Always give your dog permission to leave your side with a command like "Okay." Don't worry about the leash being between their legs; if you maintain slack in the leash, they will work around it. Since the dog has so much room, they will tend to take it all from you eventually, either in a dead run or an uncomfortable walk. When they do so, you're now in a position to call your dog for the first time. This first command to teach your dog illustrates one of the benefits of the long leash.

TEACHING "COME"

Keeping the leash low (to avoid pressure on the neck), you now reel your dog in while using an energetic voice to coax him or her to you. Then you keep reeling from the time you say "Come" to the time they're by your side. Once you've uttered the command to come, then they must come all the way to you. They can *never* disobey even a basic command as that initial inch they take will turn into a mile later on. Do not repeat yourself—this would turn a command into a plea. Reeling the dog in allows you to avoid the chance of them getting halfway to you, then seeing a squirrel and taking off again. The praise and energy displayed while reeling them toward you is important. Upon arrival, food or praise can be used as a reward. I recommend both initially.

In their mind, we want the reward for coming to register more powerfully than the most challenging distraction. They should understand where that reward comes from, whether they're far away or nearby.

You then repeat the process by giving the slack back to the dog and seeing how far they venture off. You will then set a boundary in your mind and call the dog back when they exceed that boundary. Recall can never be done too often. You as the trainer will notice their desire to leave your side dissipate over time like letting air out of a balloon. It just takes patience and repetition. It's a basic Pavlovian concept that a food reward for something a dog hates will soon turn them toward loving that thing they once despised. That's why whenever I see a good behavior I reward it, even if it's not one I specifically requested from the dog. Reward the good; distract from or ignore the bad.

Calling a dog away from something they want is the surest distraction you can create. It's important to understand that preventing the dog from making a mistake is not the goal. You want to present a temptation to the dog and then, through repetition, get them to a point where they no longer have a desire to pursue the temptation. It's a desensitization process. The more mistakes the dog makes on a long leash is just one less they will be making when you take that leash off.

TEACHING "STAY"

When walking the dog, make it a point to stop at curbs, doorsteps, and doormats on their way into the house. Each time you stop the dog, say "Stay." You will then say "Okay" after the dog has relaxed in place, releasing them from the obligation of staying. It's not important for the dog to "Sit." The concept of staying has absolutely nothing to do with "Sit." It's common for obedience trainers to have the dog automatically sit upon stopping but I don't want the dog doing anything implied. I only want the dog to do what I specifically request. These stopping points lead us into a very important part of our training—the Mark.

The Mark

The concept of "Stay" is a very vague one when you first introduce it to a dog. My father spent hours and hours having dogs "Stay" when I was growing up. He didn't use a mark, though. I learned that from another highly accomplished Hollywood trainer, Karl Miller. I adopted it because I felt it was easier for a dog to learn initially. A "mark" is simply a defined place on the floor or ground where the dog will stay—like an invisible corral. It can be a bed, a towel, a rug, a tile floor, grass, or about anything that has a surface different than the adjoining surface. A perfect example is keeping your dog on the lawn, but not going onto the sidewalk. Another example would be your dog staying on their bed at dinner time rather than begging. Staying on the curb is actually a mark, albeit one that's defined by its height and not its "feel." My experience has proven that once a dog knows a mark, then staying anywhere becomes easier. "Sit" and "Lie down" can be added later, but make them proficient on the mark/stay before introducing them to simple tricks.

If you have identified your mark we can go through the process. Let's use the doggy bed in the kitchen as our example of a mark. You're sitting down to dinner, and let's say your dog normally hangs out under the table or wanders around waiting for a handout. This would be a situation where you put on the collar and short leash prior to dinner. Reminder: We're using the short leash because we're indoors and want to avoid the leash wrapping around the dinner table. This is when we designate the spot where the dog will reside until everyone has finished eating. We start by placing the dog on the bed and saying "Stay." We want to incorporate a hand signal in our training. When you're calling them, it's a wave with your hands toward you. The hand signal for "Stay" is simply a hand extended, palm toward the dog. Keep your hand in the dog's eye line so they can see the signal easily. You would only give the command to stay when you

leave the dog and when you reward the dog; don't keep saying it in between. If you're using the hand signals from the beginning, you'll eventually be able to eliminate verbal commands altogether.

CHOOSING THE CORRECT COLLAR

Now that we've discussed the long leash—our primary training tool—the next question is what kind of collar is the best to use? There are many options regarding collars, but there are three I recommend.

While my grandfather used chain collars for all his dogs, I've adopted a couple of variations of this collar, though the principle is the same. But when it comes to the majority of larger dogs, I typically use the same collar Rudd used—a chain collar.

However, for smaller dogs or more delicate larger dogs I might use a nylon slip collar or Martingale collar. The reason I use these is they're about the only collars that release when the dog isn't pulling and tighten only when they actually pull. This ensures that the dog isn't accidentally punished for doing something correctly. There is

a specific way a collar like this should be put on.

The image to the right shows you how to place this collar correctly on your dog. The first step is to take the length of the collar and push it through either ring until the rings touch. If you walk the dog on your left, the rings should be on the left as you're facing the dog. The rings should be on the right if you prefer walking your dog on the less traditional side.

Facing the dog, the top of the collar should be a straight line and the bottom curved, like a smile. The rings should be on the left if walking on the left and on the opposite side when walking on the right. The reason we do this is to prevent the collar from locking accidentally after it tightens. It's very simple once you get used to it as you always have a 50 percent chance of putting it on right. I typically put the collar on first and then attach the leash.

It's helpful to guide the dog into the collar using food if there is any resistance, since we want the dog to look forward to being collared. We also want the dog to wear the collar and leash in any training situation, until the dog has mastered good behavior while wearing them. We want the dog to believe that the mere appearance of the leash and collar means good behavior will be enforced.

When you're in the house or taking your dog on a car trip, you can use the short leash with the training collar. It's a bit impractical to use a fifteen-foot leash in places where it could trip someone or get caught on furniture. However, the instant your training becomes an outdoor session, that's your cue to switch back to the longer training leash. In review, we have a training collar and two versions of a training leash: one for close quarters and one for greater distance.

The reason the collar and leash are so important for training is you never want to correct the dog with your hands. If you have no leash on the dog, then you will have to pursue the dog for bad behavior which personalizes the correction. When you personalize the correction, your best friend begins to react to you rather than the tools you're using. This can lead to a dog that's hand-shy or who cowers when corrected. I always tell my clients, "The hands are for love; the leash for training."

How long must we keep the leash and collar on during these training situations? My father used to tell me, "The collar and leash come off when the dog is fully trained." This means that until the dog is perfect "on leash" then he or she can't come off it unless alone or confined.

DISTRACTION TOOLS

Now that we've discussed the two essential training tools, we must talk about "distraction tools." I personally always carry something in my pocket that can get a dog's attention right away when they become overstimulated, thus "distracting" them. This distraction tool could be car keys or a favorite toy, anything that could be tossed near them to take their mind off something else.

I also carry an extra "throw-chain," which is simply a chain collar I carry in my pocket. The key to using your distraction tool is to toss it toward them when they don't see you throwing that chosen object. They should believe that it comes from an unknown location and has unlimited range—like it just fell out of the sky. The dog will actually believe this if you never throw it at them when they're looking at you.

THE TOOLS I DON'T TYPICALLY USE—AND WHY

The first time I stepped onto a movie set in 1987, I came armed with the only training tools and methods I had ever known: those learned from my pioneer dog training family. I'll admit now that I wasn't the expert trainer I thought I was at the tender age of twenty-three; though my background gave me a head start on most other trainers in the industry.

Any lack of "on-set" experience I may have had then was balanced by a deep understanding of dogs and a simple set of tools that I used in training them. Since we've already looked at the tools I use for training, let's now look at the tools I don't carry in my training tackle box.

Since each dog is different and has different needs, I would never advise a pet owner to give up a training tool that has proven to work for one of their dogs. However, don't take for granted that because a tool worked on an earlier dog, it will work on your present dog. It may, or it may not.

First, I want to mention the "hot" dog training items on the market and discuss which have limited use and which serve no practical training purpose whatsoever. All of these training items I have either tried personally or seen used on other dogs. Let's start with the tools that I believe serve no purpose at all.

The Retractable Leash

This item has become very popular, though the reason has nothing to do with their value as a training tool. They were created to make walking a dog easier for their owner, without teaching the dog much at all. I often joke with my clients that these leashes should be marketed with a cell phone since they're normally used by their owners in conjunction with one. Its value is in enabling their owner to pay less attention to their dog as they walk.

While they do allow more space for a dog to roam on leash, they don't offer the same control as a regular long training leash. They give the dog space for sniffing and marking but don't give you control when you want the dog to return. Since I often place dogs on a long leash to teach them recall, I've found the big bulky handle on the retractable leash to be an obstacle in my training. I also find that dogs can often chew through the cloth part of the retractable, making it unreliable when dealing with a dog with "leash aggression." Most of the dogs who have attempted to attack me or my canine students at a park or neighborhood came from an owner using a retractable leash.

When training dogs on the street, I avoid dogs on retractable leashes as they tend to be the most poorly behaved dogs I encounter. When there's more than one dog being walked on the retractable leash, the dogs tend to take up all the space dogs passing from the other direction would need. The plastic handle can also be a magnet for germs and can become a weapon when being dragged by a running dog. I'm certainly not alone in my assessment of these leashes as a training tool. Most professional trainers would agree with me.

When my clients ask me about using a retractable leash, I simply tell them they're fine to use—*if* your dog is already trained. As a trainer I have more control with a standard training leash, and control means everything.

The "Gentle Leader"

When talking about the gentle leader we have to place it side by side with what I use instead: the chain collar. There's a lot of talk about the humanity of using something many refer to as a "choke chain." Most of my clients find the chain collar so benign as to forget it's on their dog when I'm using it. The reason they forget is because I don't use the chain collar offensively; I allow the dog to create their own correction in a way that puts the pressure on the chest and not the neck. This requires keeping your leash hand parallel to the dog's spine.

I don't apply corrections; I simply allow them to occur naturally based on how much resistance is offered by my canine student. The fact I never have the leash higher than the dog's neck during training means I never get the "hanging" effect that gives the chain collar its bad name.

The humane aspect of the chain collar lies in the skill of the person using it. The other great thing about the chain collar is that it's more versatile than the "gentle leader." The gentle leader is really

just a walking tool. It isn't conducive for long stays or recall because it places pressure on a less stable part of the dog's body: their muzzle. Most regular collars go on a dog's neck for the same reason: stability.

When a correction is applied to a dog during my training, it's the body I'm correcting, not their head. The gentle leader forces the dog's head to turn on recall; even if their body is going the other way. This would cause concern in that a fragile dog could hurt its neck if the correction is applied improperly.

Since it isn't very durable, a stronger dog might break the thin fabric with one good pull. That would rarely happen with a metal chain collar. I imagine there's a minority of dog owners who have achieved a nice "Heel" with this device, and that's great. However, I don't use it due to its lack of versatility as a training tool and its lack of strength as a distraction deterrent.

Don't get me wrong—these two items can be useful for dogs that walk well and already have strong basics. I just can't justify their use as a training tool. My recommendation is to train the dog first before investing in either of these items.

On the other hand, the following items have achieved results—but only when conventional methods have failed. I've spoken to many a trainer who has achieved success using one or more of these training items but, overall, the reviews I've received are mixed.

Let's take a look at some of these commonly used items.

The Pinch Collar

There are many owners and trainers who swear by this item, even if it's only worked for a minority of their dogs. It's kind of a hit-or-miss training accessory, depending on your dog's sensitivity. I don't typically use them as a training tool; though I'd have considered it had I seen them working for obedience on a more consistent basis. I think they may have some use in the way of very specific behavior modification like barking or jumping deterrence for certain breeds. Most of the breeds they seem to work the best for are the larger, high-energy, short-haired dogs like Malinois, Dobermans, Rottweilers, Pit Bulls, and Mastiffs. I'm aware police departments use them for containment

during canine attack training—certainly a skill that doesn't fall under "basic obedience."

The pinch collar is looked upon by law enforcement as a strong deterrent for a dog that's overstimulated by something—like a man waving an attack sleeve—without inhibiting their desire to get it. The harness is used for the actual attack as it encourages pulling, as with a pack of sled dogs. Note: Since harnesses encourage pulling, it would not be good for canine containment. If the police department used a chain collar for attack work, the dog might lose interest in attacking; not something conducive to their goals.

When I worked in the film industry I often doubled for an actor when the scene called for a dog attack. The trainer releasing the dog on me used a chain collar but he hooked the leash to the inner ring of the collar. This way when the dog pulled—signaling their readiness to go—the collar didn't tighten. We never needed pinch collars due to the chain collars' versatility. My clients prefer to not have their dogs pulling for any reason.

I could go on about all the reasons I prefer a chain collar but the bottom line is I feel the pinch collar is too uncomfortable for a dog to wear on a regular basis, unless performing a specific behavior. I often have my clients keep their dog's chain collars on throughout the day initially, unless the dog is unattended. There is no discomfort in wearing a chain collar casually unless a correction is applied manually.

I feel it's very important to regulate corrections; I never want them happening by accident—and this could happen with a pinch collar. If you're inclined to use a pinch collar, hire someone familiar with their proper use. It should not be looked upon as a cheap alternative to hiring a professional trainer.

Also keep in mind that pinch collars are normally *only* used for larger and/or stronger dogs, not the smaller or more delicate ones that might require a lighter alternative like a slip collar or martingale. They also don't work particularly well on long-haired dogs since the prongs tend to pull the dog's hair unintentionally. I have even heard clients tell me that they worked in the beginning but their dog built up a tolerance to it.

Keep in mind that the goal in our training is to eventually eliminate the need for a leash and chain collar so the tools alone cannot be expected to do the work for you. The dog will eventually need to work as well without the collar as with it. The pinch collar would need to be left on basically forever, assuming it worked that long.

The Electronic or Shock Collar

There are many versions of these shock collars. Some stimulate good behavior through electric current; others by vibration. Some are activated by barking, some by crossing an invisible boundary, while others are initiated manually using a remote. I would never recommend any of these devices. In fact, I could only envision their use after all conventional training tools have proven unsuccessful and the only

alternative is sending the dog to a shelter. I want the dog to stay in the home.

My goal as a trainer has always been to allow bad behavior to improve organically; not force it to change. If the training tool available is something that could damage a dog's disposition, I just won't use it under any circumstances. You have to ask yourself what other problems may emerge later, even if you correct the original problem.

It's a question I ask myself every time I begin the behavioral modification process with a canine student. The entire concept of the shock collar is one I attempt to simulate with my distraction tools. Unlike the "throw-chain," the shock collar doesn't allow the dog to make the right decision; it simply intimidates them from making the wrong one. Then, upon removing the collar, the original problem reemerges. This problem could be barking, running away, aggression—whatever.

This method might seem expedient to the average dog owner but the side effects are not worth the easy fix. You might even create aggression or anxiety that didn't exist before using this collar. Since my job is to correct any obedience or behavior issues, I try not to replace problems with different ones.

Using a shock collar would make me feel responsible for any additional bad behavior that might crop up later. I feel so strongly about not using these that I won't train a dog that already has been wearing a shock collar. I feel it puts me under increased risk of being bitten during the course of the dog's training. I've only been bitten by three dogs in my fifty-five years on this earth because I don't do anything to dogs that would cause them to distrust me; anything that I would be unwilling to endure myself.

Fairness is a big part of my training—like an agreement—rather than making the dog succumb to my force or my devices. I won't proclaim that these collars don't get results because I know that they have, but at what cost? Nuclear bombs have worked, but I don't want to go to war with my dog.

It just takes a bit more patience and time to administer a humane process. I've not been forced to use one because my clients are typically willing to take the extra time it may require to teach recall or stop barking the right way. As always, if you're using a shock collar due to laziness, it's probably the wrong thing for your canine companion. Once again if you feel compelled to use this device, please seek the advice of a trainer who has experience using them.

Puppy Pads

Naturally, I work with many puppy owners in my dog training practice. Many of them have or currently use puppy pads when I arrive for their first housebreaking lesson. The sales pitch for these pads says that puppies will just magically pee on these small squares.

My clients with smaller dogs seem to have greater success using them than those with larger dogs. The biggest reason for this is the larger puppies often miss the pads, leaving much of their pee or poop on your floor.

Since these pads typically contain a scent that actually attracts puppies to them, they often end up being chewed and even swallowed by a teething puppy. Some puppies choose not to use them at all. The bottom line is they aren't magical. Being "old school" as I am, I continue to use newspaper—the same thing my dog training mentors used—in teaching housebreaking. In an upcoming chapter on puppy training, I'll go into the entire process from beginning to end.

NEW PRODUCTS

There are new products arriving on the pet scene seemingly every day. Most are just variations of accessories already in use. It's easy for a consumer to get caught up in the next "awesome" dog training tool. While product advertising is a powerful incentive, it pales in comparison to a simple repeatable process. If you consistently use certain training items on a regular basis, you're going to become an expert in their use no matter what tools they may be. You'll also naturally become comfortable with those tools on an emotional level, without hesitation prior to use or regret afterward. There are many quality trainers out there who themselves feel very comfortable with the tools they use in their training, even if they differ from those that I use. The task they have is in selling that tool to their clients for use every day. Many of my clients mention feeling good about the training I offer. Many of them have had other trainers who made recommendations that weren't comfortable for them. Therefore, no matter how close your horse gets to the water, there is no guarantee they will drink. It isn't enough that my clients know what I'm doing, they also need to know why.

I'm not just a trainer—I consider myself a relationship coach. The owners need to feel comfortable with the process. This is why I typically go to my clients' homes or wherever they experience problems, so that they can witness the training process. It allows me to teach them as well as their dog and it allows me to witness any behavioral issues in the home as they occur.

Sending a dog away on a board and train program may improve the dog's overall behavior, but it can't simulate specific behavioral triggers. The household dynamic takes on a personality of its own that normally cannot be duplicated on foreign turf. While the dog needs to adapt to the training tools being used, so must the owner. If the roles were reversed and it were me hiring a trainer, I would want to know what training tools and techniques were being used on my dog. I don't want there to be any secrets or doubts when it comes to my dog's training process or treatment. Transparency is vital to the majority of my clients.

Spending nearly every waking day of my childhood witnessing Rudd and my father train dogs was an enormous luxury. There was so much information available to me that other trainers didn't have access to until much later in their lives. Being the sponge I was as a kid, I would imitate them by teaching our own family dogs the tricks I saw them training with their movie dogs. Later, when I began working for my father as a professional trainer, I would often ask him why he trained a trick a certain way. His answer was always "figure it out." My goal is to give you access to these training techniques without having to figure it out on your own.

CHAPTER FIVE

HELPFUL HINTS IN DOG TRAINING

The art of raising puppies is basically the same as raising children under the age of four. They have to be guided constantly until it becomes habit. Then they begin to believe that good behavior wasn't forced upon them but rather that it empowers them to make the right choices themselves.

I grew up watching dog training that was based on motivating the dogs to *want* to do the right thing. Good behavior comes from consistently rewarding good behavior, even if you didn't always ask for it. If they aren't doing the right thing, punishment doesn't ensue. I simply discard it and give no value to the action. Bad behavior unrewarded is eventually perceived as a waste of time by your puppy or dog.

As a child, I would much rather have been spanked by my parents than to be ignored by them. You don't have to reward good behavior forever; just until it becomes a habit. You want to get your dog addicted to what occurs when there's good behavior on their part. The beautiful thing about dogs is how easy they are to pattern.

When I worked dogs on the set of a television show, I always needed to be consistent in my approach. If a dog was scripted to walk down the stairs, turn right around the couch, and then jump on the chair, I needed for my dog to see me walk the same route to the chair.

Then, once they knew the route, it simply became a matter of them jumping in the chair. Once they know that route they won't deviate from it; even when you do. They don't rationalize like we do.

Here is an example my father would always use when I was growing up: When a person runs into a chair, he or she thinks *what idiot put that chair there?* When a dog runs into that same chair, they think *bad chair, better stay away from those.* It's the way you saw things as a child before politics, religion, and opinions began forming your value system. This is the power you have as a dog owner, especially when they're very young. You have so much influence in the way the dog not only behaves but also what kind of personality they will have. You want that personality to be one that accepts all new places, new people, new dogs, cats—just to name a few things—with eagerness.

I often offer a toy when the dog is tempted to chew so it can teeth on that instead of something more valuable—like a couch or a child's doll. For this reason, I often put the puppy's own toys away after they become bored with them. This makes it more exciting when they're revealed suddenly as a distraction from the thing you don't want them to chew. This gives the dog an alternative rather than saying "you can't chew." They're less resistant when given options. When I was a small child, I would redirect a puppy biting by placing one of their own limbs into their own mouth so they themselves could feel the sharpness of their own teeth.

The pet owners I work with are generally made of good stuff. Most of them have very good instincts with their dogs and truly care about their pet's well-being. They're punctual when it comes to vaccinations and are generous in feeding their dog quality food. Toys are plentiful and their drinking water fresh. Many have even managed to teach some really cute tricks that they enjoy showing me during our initial home training sessions.

I then ask a couple of questions of my own like, "Does your dog come when called?" I don't normally get a confident reply from my clients as they respond with answers like "sometimes." I ask them if their dog can "Stay." Their answer is equally weak as they often say it depends upon how many people are around or whether it's morning or night.

This way of thinking is a bit backward. What good are parlor tricks when the basics haven't been mastered? Your dog may be able to do a lot of wonderful things but nothing that will ultimately protect them from an untimely death. However, teaching them a quality recall ("Come") and "Stay" will give the trainer immeasurable confidence while protecting the dog from ending up in the middle of a busy intersection.

START SOFT

Whether you're working with a large dog, a small dog, a male, or a female, my approach is the same. I start out using the soft touch and gradually make it firmer. This way I can gauge the dog's reaction to the "bunny slopes" before I put them in the Giant Slalom. You just can't go wrong that way. You won't have to retrace previous steps because your initial approach started too harsh for that particular dog.

Assessing your dog before training them is always the right move. Knowing what motivates and discourages your dog is knowledge you need to be an effective trainer. This chapter is designed to give you a general idea of what to expect—no matter what size or gender your dog may be.

There are too many trainers who train a naturally great dog early in their career, then assume all other dogs will be equally gifted. Every dog should be looked upon as a project early on, then adjusted according to their personal accomplishments.

Never stereotype dogs based on size or breed. Not all dogs are created equal. All Golden Retrievers aren't born swimmers. All Pit Bulls aren't born killers. I've worked with some great Pit Bulls in the film industry, very gentle male and female souls. In general, they aren't good rescue choices as their baggage can often include aggression. Every bit of their history should be known before adoption. Pit Bulls are best raised from puppyhood, as any flaws can be easily nipped in the bud. They need to be raised with fairness and love, more so than other breeds. By design, they're fighting dogs so we can only use kindness in order to rescue them from themselves.

As owners and trainers, we have a say in what we want our dogs to be. There are no deficiencies that can't be improved, even if not always completely eliminated.

I fix dogs every day, big and small. There have been many canine students who were headed back to the shelter before I first put my leash on them. Later the clients reminisce about how bad their dogs *used* to be. These dogs represent my greatest accomplishments. It's very rare that I'm called upon to train dogs with already solid dispositions.

The dogs I work with have bitten people, fought with other dogs, and destroyed personal property. While my father and grandfather are better known for getting a dog to save people, I'm a dog behaviorist first. I'm not here to get dogs to rescue people; I'm here to allow owners to save dogs. The only way I can do that is to make the process of acquiring a dog as seamless as possible.

The Weatherwax family is very spoiled, going all the way back to my great-grandfather Walter. We just aren't used to having dogs run our lives. My older daughter, Jean, once told me that it annoys her when she encounters poorly behaved dogs since she's so used to them being trained. There's no reason why you can't have the same expectations. Training and dogs go together like peanut butter and jelly. Just remember to properly assess your dog before you begin training them. That's always the winning combination.

LEARN TO READ YOUR DOG

Early on, you will need to learn to "read" your dog. Try to see within their eyes and their body movements and interpret their state of mind. There isn't any way to master this talent unless you work at it. That takes time and commitment. Take note of previous problem situations and bust through them with reward, not discipline. Turn the bad into good and make the exciting seem routine. The clinical term is "desensitization." I call it "what doesn't kill you makes you stronger." First a dog must endure before they can feel secure.

Try not to put expectations on your new dog based on the memories of a dog you once had. You're not replacing a former dog. You're starting over with a new dog.

I can't count the number of times clients have said to me, "My previous dog never had these problems." You must remember that "This dog is *this* dog." He might be better in some ways, worse in others. One may have had a more pleasant upbringing or may be a different breed or size. You might have even raised the prior dog and the new dog differently without realizing it. Like when raising kids, you tend to do a better job the second time around, even when the challenge is greater.

TRAINING ACCORDING TO SIZE (AND GENDER)

Training may vary according to the size and the gender of the dog.

The first time I make contact with a prospective client, there are a number of questions I ask before taking them on. Typically, I inquire about the dog's age, sex, breed, and any valid and/or known background information along with any problems the owners are already aware of. Every piece of information I receive about the dog makes me better prepared to commence my training and/or behavioral modification goals upon arrival. From that initial conversation, I'll have a fairly good idea of what reception I can expect from the dog and what tools I'll be using to train them.

I'm not the type of trainer who comes in to give a straight lecture to the clients on the first appointment. I typically strive to put a training leash and collar on the dog within the first fifteen minutes of my initial lesson. I believe my clients will learn dog training better by seeing it done and I'm not out to waste their time without an actual live demonstration. Only after the owner truly grasps the logic behind my approach will I put the leash back into their hands. Watching other trainers as I grew up is how I learned and I've found that my clients learn the same way. I'm not there to make them do my work; I'm there to get them to a point where managing their dog no longer seems like work.

Since I've already inquired about the breed of the dog, I have a relatively good idea of the size of the dog. Purebreds are easy to gauge since I've worked with every breed at one time or another. The only variable is gender, since purebred males are typically a bit larger than their female counterparts. The size of a mutt may be a little tougher to gauge from a phone call and there may be some occasions when the canine combination is so broad as to make a difference. For instance, a Dalmation/Chihuahua combination—that leads me to ask for more information regarding the dog's size so I can estimate how large a collar I may need and how durable it should be.

The size of the dog is often more important to me than the breed. While knowing the breed will tell me some of the dog's tendencies, nothing prepares me better for training than knowing the dog's size. Size can play a large part in determining the general disposition and training needs of a particular dog.

Hints for Training Small Dogs

I've enjoyed a style advantage training small dogs for one simple reason: I'm a very soft-handed trainer. Heavy-handed techniques simply don't work well for small dogs. The goal with all little fellas is to make them feel bigger. It's their size that leads to so many small dogs having a bit of the "little dog complex." This can lead those small dogs to bark at people and things excessively in order to feel bigger. It can also lead dogs to cower or run in hopes of avoiding an unpleasant confrontation. Whether they run or "project," neither is a desirable trait.

When you look at the world from the ground, it's a much different place. I'm sure you remember being little and looking up at that kitchen cupboard. It doesn't seem high now, but then it was completely unreachable. There was a vulnerability to being little, almost like you could be stepped on by the big people. Then you gained confidence, not merely because you were older, but also because you got bigger. Size and confidence seem to go hand in hand with people—and with dogs.

As I've mentioned previously, the first goal of any initial dog training lesson is to introduce the dog to the concept of "Stay." Small dogs—often being more insecure than larger dogs—may feel a bit vulnerable doing this. Deep down, any insecure dog wants an exit strategy. When you take that exiting option away from a nervous or soft dog, teaching them to stay in one place can be quite challenging.

The solution lies in making the area they're staying in larger and in the case of little dogs, elevated. Giving a small dog a higher vantage point will always make them feel more confident in one location.

Places I normally put small dogs include the top of a staircase, a tree stump, or an abandoned piece of furniture. Now they have the illusion that they're not only safer, but also more intimidating. Size is all relative to a dog compared to their surroundings. Dogs don't gaze into mirrors so they aren't aware of their own size; just their size in relation to everything else.

During my freelance movie dog training days I often assisted legendary Hollywood trainer Karl Lewis Miller. Before the cameras rolled, Karl would go to the dog's starting mark for the coming scene. Based on the size of the canine star he was working, Karl would kneel down so his height simulated that of the dog. Some crew thought this ritual silly, but I found it simply brilliant. Karl wanted to see if there were any distractions the dog would see that we as humans may not from a standing position. Was there a shiny board reflecting into the dog's face? Was the ground under the dog too hot? What better way to determine these factors than to be the dog for a moment?

Perception is everything when working with dogs. If a dog thinks the world is dangerous, no explanation on your part will change their mind. No matter how unreasonable you may consider the fear, it can be very real to your canine partner with short legs. The goal is to alter that perception. Elevating a little dog will even the playing field from their point of view. This will lead to a more secure dog. A secure dog will be more focused and attentive to commands.

The best trainers I've ever known have elevated their little dogs. Legendary trainer Frank Inn trained two generations of Benji using a small table on his wheelchair. When training little dogs for movies, my family normally trained them using standard-sized tables. You can also use a chair or a step but the higher we can get the dog, the better. We want the dog to have stability wherever we put them so the elevated surface needs to be stable and give the dog traction.

Training dogs for more than three decades, I've done my share of bending over. It can take its toll on your body. Training your small dog on a raised surface will mean less bending over for you. The easier your approach to training, the more likely it is to continue. Even trained dogs will need practice from time to time. Like the saying goes, "use it or lose it." Training should be part of a dog's entire life.

Training a small dog on an elevated, broad surface like a table will also make your angle less intimidating to the dog. Whether you're praising or correcting your little guy, it will be accepted with less hesitation from a more even eye level. Coming over the head of a little dog can be quite intimidating when you're six feet tall and your student is standing twelve inches off the ground.

After they've learned all their basics on that table, you can bring them back to the ground and develop distance on your stay and recall. Look at the table like training wheels when learning to ride a bike—it makes it easier in the beginning but eventually you no longer need them.

Once your little dog is working from a distance they'll no longer view your height advantage the same way since you'll no longer be towering over them from two feet away. A little dog with confidence will not need to be touched by hand unless you're praising them. If the dog has strong basics, then the leash and the side of your foot can be used to correct any mistakes they might make. The general theme of my training has always been focused on using the hands primarily for praise anyway.

Hints for Training Large Dogs

Training a large dog is an entirely different situation. There's no need for elevation since their head is already waist level or higher. Where I may feed a small dog from my pants pocket, I will typically raise the eye level of a large dog to that of a shirt pocket.

I can't talk enough about the power of distance with all dogs since they all need to develop isolation skills. It's nice that our dogs love us but we don't want them to be dependent on constant close contact with us. This means we will use a long leash and immediately set boundaries.

The table we used for our small dog is a boundary in itself but for large dogs we'll use clear ground boundaries like a patch of grass or a curb. Using our long leash, we will always have control of our dog, even if they're some distance from you. Remember Stay-and-Recall is all about distance.

Getting a big dog to heel is a little different. If you're using a "tight heel" the dog should be close enough to your preferred side that your legs can come into play. While you'll be using your leash to keep your dog from pulling, you will use your body to keep the dog on the proper side. A gentle shove with your leg when your dog crowds you will teach them to respect your space and pay better attention to your commands. The mere fact that you're not using your hands will make your correction seem like magic to them. Remember than any leash corrections you make won't have the goal of lifting the dog, only slowing them. This means leash corrections will force the dog to slow, not be taken off the ground.

Using your body weight whenever possible with a big dog sends the message that you won't be bullied. You must send a clear message that you will be using every training tool in your arsenal. It could be your hip, your leg, or your elbow—but it certainly can't be your hands. While you'll be searching for parity with your small dog, you'll be emphasizing more dominance and control with most large dogs.

Whether you're doing a tight heel or a loose one, your body speed and weight should be controlling the dog's distance and speed. If you're swinging your arms around, you're simply not being efficient. If you keep your leash hand close to your hip then it will be your body that stops them. If you feel any strain on your arms or hands, place the leash behind your waist and let your body serve as an anchor. This way your arms aren't doing the work; your body weight is.

This is the way it works with the more confident large dogs. Then there are the "softer" large dogs, who are a lot more like our small dogs. They may look like a large dog but see themselves as something smaller. They're more sensitive to correction than the typical big guy.

My collie, Prince, is one of these gentle giants. Through exposure he learned to fear nothing, except a harsh word or excessive correction. If my power dial is at 10 for a confident dog, I turn it down by about 50 percent with a dog like Prince. Many collies tend to be sensitive, which goes a long way to explaining why I have such a soft touch as a dog trainer.

Like the little dog, our big softie needs confidence far more than discipline. These dogs are already afraid of making mistakes so we will emphasize their accomplishments more while their mistakes are basically thrown away. The best way to give a dog confidence is to put them in a situation where they can easily be successful. We might want to move slower with their training and exposure. Everything will be done in baby steps. They may be easier to train than the confident dog, but that's of little use if they're too focused on what could potentially hurt them.

I won't focus as much on control with the softer big dog. Since confidence is what they need, distance is more useful than control. They tend to be clingy, much like many little dogs, so we will seek opportunities to build physical separation from us. These less confident dogs always seem to learn "Come" quicker since they're a bit more subservient than the braver dog. If we're using the brake more with the outgoing dog, we'll use the accelerator more with the shier, less stubborn dog.

Whether you have a small dog or a "soft" big dog, they can change over time. Many of the shy dogs that I train end up morphing into the confident dog. This means the delicate approach we may have chosen initially could change, calling for more rigid enforcement later. We want our training approach to evolve in sequence with the dog's mental evolution. If you were using the accelerator in the early phases of training, you may end up relying more on the brakes later on.

TIME AND DISTANCE

Growing up and working in the film industry, I learned that there are two factors in training that overshadow everything else: Time and Distance. It isn't enough that your dog can stay while you stand three feet in front of your dog for a duration of thirty seconds to a minute. That's a good start, but you always want to keep stretching the length of time they can stay, as well as move yourself farther and farther away from the dog. Of course, this is a gradual process requiring the patience to allow your success to come naturally. The long leash will give you the confidence to leave your dog alone on a curb, a porch step, or somewhere less defined. If the long leash is under your foot you don't have to worry about the dog running off. You can start out three feet away then extend that distance over time until you no longer need a leash at all. I always feed the dog in the place they're staying and I never call a dog out of a stay. Keep "Come" and "Stay" separate as they work against one another. Instead, when releasing a dog from the "Stay" position I always use "Okay"; the same goes for any other static position like "Sit" or "Lie Down." Remember if the goal is to get your dog to work off-leash, then a short leash will never get you there.

When you first acquire your dog, it's natural that you'll want to teach them some strong basics eventually. Now replace the word "eventually" with *immediately*. Teaching your dog the guidelines as soon as they're in their new home will help you avert self-created bad habits—habits the dog didn't have upon arrival. While you'll have a regular collar for identification purposes, you'll also need to establish the training collar you want them to wear when you're in a training session. You'll attach the short leash in the home or in transit and the long leash when you're outside or in an uncontrolled situation. You will also keep the leash and collar on whenever you're home and awake. This will remain the case until the dog can be trusted without the leash and collar. It may seem cumbersome at first, but chasing your poorly behaved dog around the house or correcting them with your hand should be avoided at all costs. This is more about making your dog comfortable in their own skin than about discipline. We don't want to make any corrections detrimental to helping your dog acquire a calm disposition. My experience has shown me—in the film industry *and* in private training—the dog's fear is at the root of most bad behavior. This includes aggression toward people and other dogs, excessive barking, and running away.

So it's important in training to expose the dog to things that make them uneasy with the goal of removing their fears. The long leash works well for this as it allows the dog to leave your side to explore and to build their confidence in this big, scary world. A short leash doesn't give your dog the freedom to alleviate their fears.

When you hold a dog back (usually on a short leash) it actually has the reverse effect of making them more uptight and thus pulling more. Therefore, when you're walking your dog you should shorten your leash only when the part dragging behind you could get caught on a person or objects like sprinklers, trash cans, or car tires.

When you have open area, let the dog take the full length of your long leash. When they've taken all your leash, call them back and reward them. If you repeat this enough—especially when the dog is distracted—the more reliable your recall will become. If your dog decides to dig their heels in when you call them, then you may have to create momentum by running away from the dog while holding the leash. Then when we've worn the dog out—by leaving you and coming back—the dog will be more confident while taking less of your leash each time they drift off. Then you can transition smoothly to "heel."

Let's think of "Heel" as simply a tighter walk where the dog is somewhere near your side. It doesn't matter which side; just be consistent. After you've done recall it's safe to say that the dog will be less inclined to pull since they've already used their frequent flyer miles trying to venture beyond the span of your leash. The first thing we want to do is shorten the leash and let the remainder drag behind you (you can always wash the leash later). The reason I don't want you to try holding all fifteen-plus feet of leash is because it will preoccupy you from being an effective trainer. Once again, think of the leash as a Cobra and you only have to control the head. Then position yourself next to the dog so that he or she is left with the side you want them to take. Then you begin to walk. The moment the dog begins to speed up, *stop*, and say "Heel" (that's the commonly used word, but I prefer the word "Easy" just because it sounds better—it's up to you which to use, but you must be consistent). The dog will acknowledge your command of "Easy" or "Heel" by looking up at you after stopping. This would be the time to feed and/or praise your dog. Then you begin to walk again and stop and reward whenever the ball begins rolling faster than you would like.

I normally teach my clients to hold some of the leash behind their back so they don't always have to use their arms alone to stop the dog. The command "Okay" would be the command to go back into "free mode" (where you give them the whole leash and let them sniff around). Going from "Okay" back to "Easy" or "Heel" is only a matter of calling the dog back to you—and rewarding—and then assuming the position we took when beginning heel. "Heel" and "Stay" are used to teach the dog boundaries. This is important because dogs function much better with structure in their lives.

THE IMPORTANCE OF TOUCH, TALK, & TONE (TT&T)

All of us are familiar with the power of dynamite. We know that it's dangerous. Those who handle explosives in their occupations are extremely well versed on its volatility. These individuals know that taking shortcuts can lead to dire consequences. Practicing a consistent process is not only safer but is also easier to remember since we've never done it any other way. Dog training also calls for a predictable and consistent approach, especially from the canine student's point of view.

Every dog is unique. There are big ones, small ones, purebreds, and mutts. Since they form such a diverse group it makes consistency in training all the more important. The elements that bring about a well-behaved dog often go beyond pure obedience and training. It also comes in *how* you're interacting with your dog. Is the contact you make with your dog during training sending the wrong message? Is there a clear delineation between work and play?

Touch is a critical element in sending the appropriate message to your dog. When you're playing with your dog it's natural to hug, pet, and tease them. Touch is part of the game and it should have a motivating effect. Some dogs react more positively to contact than others, but there's no denying its overall power. Touch and praise should always go together. If you're making hand contact with your dog and it's not for praise or play, then it's probably not appropriate. This is why we use the leash for training and not for play.

The leash takes the personal part out of any correction. It also clearly signifies when play has ended. When that leash goes on it tells the dog "good behavior will now be expected." It also minimizes any perceived trauma a dog may internalize when you're forced to initiate a correction. If we were to use our own hands for that correction it would be like saying "I disapprove of you" as opposed to "this is incorrect." It's much like the difference between saying to a child "you're stupid" as opposed to telling them that what they did was wrong. We want to always be conscious of sending messages that don't destroy canine self-esteem.

In the process of restricting use of the leash to corrections alone, we transfer more power to our hands as a reward tool. It makes the hands' role very specific—and potentially explosive. Sometimes that combustibility is an asset while at other times it works against you.

If you're calling your dog, the expectation of a physical (hand) reward normally only expedites their return to you, making it an asset. The hands serve as a target to them in this situation. Like a catcher's mitt to a pitcher. Since they've never had a reason to fear the hands, there are no mixed signals given and a clear and positive target is provided. Conversely, the memory of your hands in a past physical correction when called can only bring about doubts as to the outcome of their returning this time.

If your goal is to keep your dog from breaking a "Stay," then the hands can become a huge liability. Depending on the dog and the breed, merely touching them when "on stay" can send the message that you're either done or are about to be asked to do something else. This means the mere act of praising them physically can get them to break their stay. In some dogs, physical praise is equivalent to putting gasoline on a fire. This is where the food reward is more effective. While dogs enjoy food rewards, it doesn't require touching their body to do it. If using a leash is the neutral correction, then using food is the neutral reward, except when in the presence of other dogs.

Using a timely food reward—just for good behavior—encourages that particular behavior to continue. The use of a hand reward in the same situation normally results in excessive enthusiasm from the dog, leading to decreased calmness and control. While there certainly are some very calm dogs that can handle physical praise while on a stay, less praise typically works better.

My experience also tells me that the short-haired dogs tend to have greater reactions to physical praise than the longer-coated dogs. It's seemingly like their nerves are closer to the skin. Many long-haired dogs are numbed to their surroundings by their massive coats. These thick locks often obstruct their vision and hearing, making them less aware of any potential distractions. Small dogs are generally more sensitive regardless of their coat than large dogs. Due to their diminutive size, they're generally a bit less comfortable in their own skin.

Then there's the question of when you're using your hands when not training. What false signals are you sending? Do your hands say "yes" when your voice says "no"? There are subtle things we do as dog owners that encourage our dogs to behave badly. The scary part is that we spend a lot more time critiquing our dogs than we do ourselves. If the opposite were true, we would shed greater light on all the mistakes we make as pet owners.

I admit it. I did it too. I had far more opportunities to make errors than the average person. The saving grace for me was there was always someone nearby possessing the knowledge to recognize my mistakes. Pointing out my errors prevented me from reinforcing bad behavior over and over again.

Take that moment you first arrive home after a long day, the only event marked on your dog's mental calendar. There are many triggers in this single event. There's the sound of your car pulling in. There are the noises you might make between the car and the front door. Then there's the jingling of the keys. All these sound cues heighten your dog's anticipation until it's at a fever pitch. Then when you reach to open the front door, it's equivalent to letting air out of a balloon. The air has to go somewhere, right? In that pivotal moment you should already be pondering whether you will have to correct or reward your dog. Most of the time we don't anticipate the good, we merely react to the bad. When we're caught by surprise and overwhelmed by the moment, we normally don't send the right message to our dog. We have to take the initiative away from the dog by being more deliberate ourselves.

Good behavior—like not jumping—will always be rewarded. The payoff should be extended down toward the dog since "down" is precisely where you want them to be. Any reward will do. Hand praise is typical in this situation, though many owners will keep dog treats near the front door for easy access. Bringing the reward to the dog's level tells them that it's the only level where food or love will be acquired. Justified rewards are even more important than justified correction, as the dog will recognize its absence when it hasn't been earned.

I can't stress enough how pivotal hand contact can be. Your dog's perception is always that hand contact is good—at least that's what it should be. If you walk through that door and you inadvertently touch their head while they're jumping, you have just rewarded jumping. If your dog is barking at a visitor to your home and you use your hands to quiet them, you have just rewarded that behavior. The leash isn't just for training, it also allows us as trainers to minimize hand contact with our dog. Minimizing hand contact equates to a dog that's not receiving mixed signals. Make sure your hands are saying the same thing your voice is saying.

When using a hip, knee, or elbow to correct your dog, he or she receives no message other than "this isn't working in my favor." If they then repeat that bad behavior, simply repeat the corresponding correction. The owner who corrects their dog once more than the dog misbehaves wins. In a committed battle of wills, the owner should always prevail. The problem is that we often aren't as dedicated to the battle as our dog. We wave the white flag far too early.

Someone once told me the only difference between the chicken and the pig when it comes to a breakfast of bacon and eggs is that the chicken is merely involved while the pig is committed. Commitment is the thing you need most when it comes to teaching strong obedience. It doesn't matter that it's a holiday or your dog is having an off day. Good training isn't circumstantial; the rules in place today are also applicable tomorrow. It's not about moods or the weather. The words "sometimes" and "maybe" just don't exist in your dog's vocabulary. The only words your best friend needs to know are "always" and "never."

This applies to good behavior as well. The reward should be offered for random good behavior, even behavior we didn't specifically request. If there was praise for good behavior yesterday, why is there none today? Recognition and correction go hand in hand. We praise our dogs to give them recognition for making good choices. Sometimes your dog simply avoiding bad behavior is justification for being rewarded. It really depends on what behavior you, as an individual, find valuable. There are certainly things that bother me about dogs that don't bother others, and vice versa.

Much of this hand contact is instinctual on our part. We might think that since contact works so well in comforting another person, it will also work for a dog. But as I've explained, dogs perceive physical comfort as approval of their current behavior. Therefore, we physically reward only normal behavior; normal by our standards. We constantly have to ask ourselves, "Is the contact I'm giving my dog at this very moment justified?" Thinking of the goal instead of the process can help you.

Tough love is the best remedy you can offer a dog in distress, no matter how uncomfortable it may be for you. We say through our silence and confident body language that the dog's fear is unfounded. Coddling an anxious dog is sending the message that this is the right way to feel. Tough love comes into play when you decide to make your dog face their fears without hesitating on your part. Never retreat from the place your dog finds most uncomfortable. If they want to run for cover, we simply prevent them from doing so with a leash. We always feed them for calmness during difficult situations since food is the neutral reward. It merely makes a questionable situation synonymous with a positive result. It doesn't weaken a dog the way physical coddling would. The food reward sends the correct message in that it's simple and easy for them to understand. The message is "every time we're in this situation, food will come." Over time the timid dog becomes braver as he begins to replace the bad feeling once associated with those previously unstable situations. Only food and a neutral (committed) attitude will bring about the erasure of your dog's fears.

The Role of Talk and Tone

The role our voice plays in everyday life is significant in the development of our dog. Just like touching your dog, the act of talking to your dog can distract them from independent thinking. I don't know how many times I've seen people walking their dog and trying so hard to get them to go to the bathroom. Then when the dog is about to go, they say "good dog" and the dog is distracted from completing the act. These moments illustrate how important it is for dogs to just figure things out. Like our touch, our voice can become a crutch in a dog's development. Too much guidance can frustrate your dog, sometimes to the point of encouraging rebellion.

If we weren't around, our dogs would find a way to survive. They would find food and water and a place to sleep. They're very resilient. In fact, about the only thing they couldn't get on their own is our companionship. The same could be said for us as humans. We become complete with a dog, as a dog does with us as owners. It's a partnership, not canine servitude.

Training a dog is like playing poker. How much talking goes on at a poker table? It's an unwritten rule not to converse with others at the table. It's the same with our attitude during training. Our talk and tone says a lot more than it seems. Some people are nervous talkers and talk simply because they can—there's no discernable purpose in their words. With your dog, your constant talk can lessen the impact of each command. The tone a nervous talker uses reveals their poker hand. The wrong tone in your voice would be telling your dog that they have a hand possibly stronger than yours. It encourages the dog to take liberties simply because they detect that you're bluffing. Like a poker player, we want to reveal as little as possible regarding our state of mind so our dog can't use any perceived weakness against us.

It's the same when on first dates. We often feel pressured to say something when we feel that uncomfortable silence. The words we force from our mouth seldom come out spontaneously. In a dog training situation, using a minimal word count is most effective. Once you've given a dog a static command like "Stay," the dog is then generally anticipating to either be released from that position or be issued another command. When silence follows a command, there's nothing to mislead a dog from continuing their current behavior.

If you're playing with your dog in a nonworking situation, voice can be used freely. Just be aware of when the play evolves into work. This is normally signified by the leash and training collar going on. Your dog should also be able to clearly recognize the difference in your demeanor. They will notice that you're more serious and your tone is brought down to a lower level. When the training leash goes on your dog, it's telling them whatever we were doing before matters not; this is time for work! Training isn't meant to be a negative, but it puts you back in charge at a time when play has naturally eroded your control.

I use a lot of strategic voice in my dog training practice. Since I would be considered a motivational trainer, I'm often striving to build confidence in dogs. The dogs lacking in natural confidence are often hearing a higher, more enticing tone from me than those possessing a surplus of self-esteem. These are the dogs we need to "speed up." This happens by overemphasizing the small achievements they make. The praise is greater and comes more often because it's what *they* need.

While a stern voice is seldom ever used with the slower, more timid dogs, it's essential with the energetic "normal" dogs. A rigid voice and posture tells the outgoing dog that you can't be manipulated. The very energetic dogs will push the envelope a bit more in training. They want to test your boundaries. It isn't because they're smarter than the slow dog, they have just had more previous positive reinforcement. They may never have had any reason to anticipate any negative consequences.

Look at the timid and the outgoing dogs like a teeter-totter. The confident canine starts out on the higher end. A low voice pulls them down. The less confident dog should be elevated. A higher voice will raise them up. We don't want a dog that's too high or the one that's too low. We want to begin from the middle. The middle is always a great place to start since it's you who then decides which direction they go from there.

Anytime you teach a dog something new, your enthusiasm should be higher than normal. A dog who receives high praise and/or a food reward will always learn quicker than one presented with no food and weak verbal praise. However, once they've learned a given command, reward should be toned down accordingly. We don't want to continue rewarding our dog for specific behaviors they've already mastered. It isn't to say we won't acknowledge the good things our dogs do, there just won't be as much fanfare attached to it.

Just like when taking your dog for a bathroom break, there are times when your voice and hand contact work against you. It's always better for a dog to be induced to perform rather than being ordered to do it. A dog takes much more satisfaction from situations where they're making decisions for themselves. We never want to break a dog's focus during the times when they're really trying to do something on their own. These rules also apply to when the dog is performing behaviors I've referred to as "static."

STATIC BEHAVIORS

There are really just two truly static behaviors: "Heel" and "Stay." They are the two commands that ask a dog to do *less*; not learn more.

While it takes patience to teach your dog new tricks, it takes even more to get them to continue doing a single thing for a very long time. Dogs hate waiting probably more than anything else. Every day is like Christmas morning for them. They always want to open the presents. While "Heel" isn't a truly static position like "Stay," both behaviors require a great deal of self-control on your dog's part.

Most dogs I've trained enjoy going on walks. It isn't something your dog has to be sold on. Keeping this in mind, I remind you to put a leash on well before the walk occurs. The leash will not only suppress some of the dog's exuberance, it will also allow you to avoid hand contact when the walk begins. The leash will be doing most of the work for you. Anything the leash doesn't control can be accomplished by guiding the dog with your body. The only words your dog will hear while on heel is the command itself. The tone should be very low and firm. The only reason you would ever elevate your voice is when the dog is fearful or needs encouragement to continue walking. A lower voice is like stepping on the brake; a high voice or hand contact is like hitting the accelerator.

Stay comes into play in nearly every phase of your dog's training. Stay is like the period to every training sentence. Every command you want a dog to perform will be followed by "Stay." If you tell a dog to "Sit" then you must follow the command with "Stay." The same applies to "Lie down" or any other static command. A dog should never be expected to improvise or read minds. Make sure you clearly express whether they're required to remain in their current position. It isn't necessary to explain anything to a dog; just let them know what they should be doing now. Dogs reside in the here and now—a place humans only visit.

Once you tell your dog to stay, there's nothing else to say. They should remain in that place until you either move them with the leash or give them the "okay" to leave. Touching or talking will not help you when your dog is stationary.

Always be mindful of what you're saying to your dog and why you're saying it. Is the tone you're using consistent with the energy level required? Is your dog performing a static command like "Stay" or an active one like "Come"? Do they need a voice tone that encourages movement or one that induces calm behavior? Are you touching your dog unnecessarily?

These are questions you should be asking yourself throughout the training process. Remember to look at the world through your dog's eyes. The key is recognizing the power of every touch, every word, and every inflection. They all mean something to your dog, even if you aren't always aware of it yourself.

Avoid any food reward for your dogs in the presence of other dogs or for simply "being cute." You might call this "strategic reward." In other words, we want to make a reward an event and only offered at the moment our request to them is fulfilled. We don't want to reward our dog for doing something they've already mastered or for nothing at all. Food reward should be reserved for real improvement. That improvement could appear in the form of performing a specific behavior or for reacting more positively in a specific situation. Needless to say, any uneasiness the dog has shouldn't be confirmed with baby talk or hand contact. When training, keep your voice level, making any change in your tone easier for the dog to recognize. It's like the "Cry Wolf" tale—if you raise your tone of voice, typically the dog will be less responsive when urgency is truly needed. In layman terms, this means "don't sweat the small stuff."

The principles of touch, talk, and tone are the building blocks to training your dog in a positive, Weatherwax way. It isn't enough to merely teach your dog tricks. Tricks don't make a better-behaved dog; however, tricks are easier to teach a dog that possesses a solid foundation.

PATTERNING

The thing I love most about dogs is how easy they are to pattern. Whatever meaning you choose to attach to a situation or person will be embraced by your dog until eradicated. If they eat their dinner in front of a bus stop, for example, they will begin to look forward to going to a bus stop. This is the same concept I use in crate training: If food and toys come from inside the crate, our dog begins to embrace being there. They will begin to reevaluate what the crate means to them based on what their payoff is. What's in it for them?

I know something about balance with dogs from my experience growing up in a movie dog training family. Most movies and television shows with animals typically have multiple trainers. Since movement for trainers is restricted on a movie set, you might need one trainer to "release" a dog and another to "receive" them. The head trainer can't be everywhere on the set at once. This also requires that the dog respond with equal sharpness to each trainer's commands. The head trainer may end up doing the most difficult part of a scene but the assistant trainers create that balance.

When my dad first began working on the Lassie series in 1963—the year I was born—he had recently returned from Army service in Germany. Grandpa Rudd was the head trainer and Sam Williamson was his first assistant. This had been the case for some time. Balance already existed between Rudd and Sam. Then, like adding a member to our household, my dad arrived on the scene.

Dad told me of his first experience working a scene on the Lassie series as a way to illustrate how Rudd would test him. It was a preview of what to expect when I began working for him.

The scene was pretty typical for the long-running show. In my dad's first scene, Lassie was supposed to look to one actor, then another, before exiting the scene. Rudd would firmly say "Stay" and Lassie would look at him. Then it was my dad's turn to pull a sharp look away from Rudd before Sam called the dog out of frame.

When Dad's turn came to "pull the look," Rudd's presence simply overwhelmed him. Rudd gave him an earful afterwards, "Dammit Robert, if you can't pull the look I can't have you on the show." This was a strong wakeup call for my dad. He devised a plan for the next time he had to pull a look from the world's greatest trainer.

The next day while walking Lassie before the first scene, Dad pulled something from his jacket: a glazed donut. While I don't recommend you do this at home, my father fed Lassie this sugary treat (fortunately, the dog didn't get sick from it). Since Dad had read the episode script, he knew there would be another scene where he would need to pull a strong look away from Rudd. This time Lassie looked so strongly toward my dad when he said "Stay," that my grandfather struggled to reclaim the look. This shocked Rudd, but was a turning point for my dad. Rudd never found out about the donut, but he quickly realized that dad might just work out as an assistant trainer.

Since this was Lassie's first donut, it had a lasting impression. Over time working on the show, that bond between my father and Lassie only became stronger. He no longer had to use smoke and mirrors to get Lassie to respond to his commands. He achieved balance by offering something Lassie never acquired anywhere else. Dad, in essence, made himself indispensable.

I never had the same issues assisting my father on "The New Lassie" because I already had a strong bond with the current Lassie before the series began shooting in 1989. I certainly remembered the stories and I wasn't going to let myself fall into the same trap.

Dogs aren't like hats or jackets. They aren't "Wash and Wear." The relationship between a person and a dog doesn't come naturally; it's cultivated over time. Whoever wants to take charge of a dog must have a relationship with that dog. I can't tell you how many times I picked up dogs well ahead of time for a movie shoot or TV show. If I had the luxury of bonding time with a new dog, I always took advantage of it. The more time I spent around the dog, the more comfortable I felt.

Spending time with the dog doesn't mean letting them do whatever they want. It's about building a partnership. We're trading services. My dog will know that I am fair, I am generous, but also that nothing will be received without receiving something in turn from them.

This is how I want you to look at your dog when training. You typically get exactly what you give. If you aren't invested in your dog, he or she won't feel committed to you. This means that if you don't value what your dog does for you, respect is hard to attain. If you're not consistent in your approach, then good behavior will be difficult to maintain. Dog training never really ends. Like a car, they must continue to get tune-ups.

Once you achieve proper behavior and balance with your dog, it's your job to exercise those skills from time to time. Dog training isn't a one-step process like riding a bike. Dog training is about both you and your dog learning and re-learning. New obstacles arrive regularly when it comes to dog ownership. It's up to you to adapt to the changes while maintaining a sense of normalcy for your dog. Dogs crave consistency.

I'm still learning something new every day when it comes to training. Like people, dogs evolve over time. A fear they have today can disappear then reappear after one negative event. By the same token, a positive event can alleviate previous trauma.

Dogs work a lot like the stock market. The market rises and falls based on a perception of the future. It isn't about what's happening now but what *could* happen later, what is likely to occur based on market expectations. Your dog is no different. You set expectations for your dog. Once expectations are set, we never lower them. If anything, we use that base of knowledge to raise expectations over time. We don't want to rest upon our foundation but build upon it one step at a time.

Drive your dog regularly. Don't let his tires get flat. Don't let the hoses crack. Above all, don't be afraid to let someone else drive him/her from time to time. While every dog needs a primary leader, begin to think about what will happen in your absence. Peace of mind is having your own training knowledge in that mental safe. The greatest peace of mind comes from knowing that someone else can unlock that safe in your absence.

WHAT ABOUT HIRING A TRAINER?

These good people become clients of mine not because they're lazy or uncaring. Quite the contrary, they do care . . . and are willing to admit they're not great at dog training, so they hire me. It's okay not to be a trainer of your dog. This book is meant to help you train your pet—but if it turns out that training your dog yourself isn't working and you need to call in a professional trainer, look for one who is "kind" to your best friend. Try to avoid any trainer who's condescending or refuses to explain why he or she is doing something a certain way. Board and Train programs can be okay if you're already familiar with your dog trainer's style. Never send your canine companion to someone who uses methods with which you are unfamiliar.

You'll need to be able to emulate the training and methods yourself at some point. I believe in being involved in my dogs' training, just as I would want to be there in their final moments of life. Training should always involve an "open-door" policy with your trainer, even if you are not present during all of your dog's training.

I am the last dog training Weatherwax. Rudd is gone and my father is long retired. It's up to me to get the word out. When I no longer walk this earth, I hope that there exists a formula for training dogs the way my family has trained for nearly a century. It's a time-tested method that isn't used by today's trainers. It's so old it's actually become new again.

When I worked in the film industry, other trainers justified their methods over ours by saying "those methods are ancient and outdated." I just told them what my grandfather always said: "The dogs haven't changed, so why should my methods?" That made a lot of sense and normally put the "ancient" word to rest.

Like the brand of dog food that Lassie once ate, this is my "Recipe" for dog training. My recipe takes a simple method of training and combines it with occasional behavior modification as needed. There are no perfect dogs and there are no perfect trainers. The key is consistency and a plan. If you combine these two things with a large dose of love, then you will succeed.

REMAIN FLEXIBLE AND KEEP ON LEARNING

I continue to learn new things on the job even after training dogs for more than thirty years. I always try to remain flexible enough to absorb new information. It seems the more I learn, the more I realize I don't know. For instance, through the years I've discovered ways to shorten training time without using more rigid techniques. I've also learned to develop alternatives to my most effective training solutions in preparation for that rare instance when one particular dog fails to respond to my primary training option. It's my goal to continue to improve my skills for as long as I train dogs.

When training your own dog, it's extremely important to learn from your training mistakes and to store new knowledge as it's attained for future use. This way you can avoid repeating procedural mistakes when training. If you're reliving mistakes previously made, then you might be sleeping at the switch.

This simply means that preoccupation could be leading you to miss visible clues. These hints are all around us. The information you actively accumulate handling and training dogs over the years will allow you to develop a sense that only experience creates: The Art of Anticipation.

CHAPTER SIX

BAD-BEHAVIOR TRAINING

Given the opportunity, virtually every dog would develop behavior that is either destructive or just plain bothersome. Consistency in training as early as possible will curb much of a dog's tendency to behave badly . . . however you, the owner, choose to define bad behavior.

There are several behaviors that most owners want their dogs to stop performing. Let's take a look at some of the most common of these bad behaviors and how to deal with them.

DOG BARKING AT DOOR OR WINDOW

This is a situation I run into often in my training and it can be an easy fix. If the dog is barking out the window at a jogger or at the door when a guest arrives, this is where you establish the distraction tool. Since this is a training situation, I would have the training collar and short leash on the dog (since we're indoors). I normally begin the desensitization process before an actual guest arrives by having someone else simulate the situation.

Say you and your daughter are in the house. You can get your daughter to ring the doorbell while you stand with a distraction tool in hand. The distraction tool you use can be anything that gets a reaction, either by the sound or vibration it makes, or what the object means to them. It could be something they love, like a toy, or something they acknowledge or respect, like car keys or a chain collar. As soon as the dog barks, you throw the object behind them. The very moment the correction tool lands, you say "No!" in a strong voice. Remember the tool must be thrown before the verbal correction, or the dog may turn around and see you throw the object, so throw before "No!" The more noise your object makes, the better.

If the sound is muffled by carpeting, then have the object hit something like the door for more effect. The moment the dog reacts to the thrown item (that the dog did *not* see you throw), be sure to praise and feed the dog.

If you apply any correction, balance it with affection. You then repeat this process by having the doorbell ring again. If there's barking, throw the distraction tool again, say "No!" firmly, wait for the dog's reaction, then praise and reward.

Eventually you'll be able to stop the barking by simply jingling the chain or keys, bouncing the ball, or squeaking their favorite toy (your distraction tool). The key is praising the dog immediately after the bad behavior ceases. This is called "a bridge," which is the point in time when the dog has achieved momentary perfection.

In essence, you're marking the good behavior in the mind of your dog. If they begin barking again, then the reward is withheld. There is no punishment for bad behavior; just reward for good behavior.

Now that you've stopped the barking, what do we do once the guests begin walking through the door? This is where the short leash may provide backup for your handheld distraction tool. Once again, the reason we have the leash is to correct jumping if the distraction tool doesn't work. We absolutely *cannot* touch the dog in this situation. Any physical correction should come from the leash. A hand correction can be misinterpreted as praise. Then look for the "bridge" again, which in this scenario would be the dog returning to all four feet after a short, snappy leash correction. That would be the time for verbal and/or food reward.

Once you've acquired your two training tools and one distraction tool, you can begin the work of modifying your dog's behavior. The tools provide all the "intimidation" you'll need in your training. It's much better to have your tools be looked upon with respect while your dog looks at *you* with love. Keep in mind that a retractable leash does not substitute as a training leash. This popular leash is for a dog that is already trained to walk well and come to you. Save that acquisition until your dog has conquered any issues he/she may have at home or in the great outdoors.

DIGGING

The interesting thing about dogs is that they don't have any reservations against putting their nose right in the thick of another dog's droppings. What's peculiar is that most dogs are much less eager to put their face in their own leavings. For this reason I've found the most effective way to control a digging dog is to put their own excrement on top of their preferred digging location. This is the "remote" method since most digging occurs after the occupants of the home have left.

However, if you're able to catch your dog in the act, the correction is more effective ensuring that they don't just seek out a new preferred digging place. The correction is best accomplished using our distraction tool. If you can throw something toward their rear legs while they are actually in the act of digging, the results will be much more far reaching than the remote method.

If you're unable to catch your dog digging, you'll just have to keep putting their poop in the holes they've already dug. Keep in mind that if you have multiple dogs, someone will have to keep track of where the offending canine has dropped their load. Dropping the wrong dog's poop in the hole won't normally deter the behavior.

BEGGING AND JUMPING ON FURNITURE

I believe that neither is bad behavior if you're okay with it. It's all about perception. Remember, "mind over matter." If you don't mind, then it doesn't matter. If it *does* matter, the key is making them wait. If your dog wants to jump on the couch, they should only be allowed to join you on the couch when you have given them permission. That's when they receive their payoff.

As for begging, when it comes to mealtime the best way to avoid begging is to put them on a separate mark and reward them for staying there. No food should come from the table. Their treats should be kept in a separate place close to where the dog is staying. Make sure that if either of these problems exists, a leash and collar must be worn by the dog so that no corrections will be personalized by using the hands.

BITING/JUMPING ON YOU

Puppies that haven't acquired their permanent teeth will be in a constant struggle to force out the baby teeth they have. This teething process tends to make you the target of some unwelcome and seemingly aggressive behavior. It isn't aggression, but rather frustration. There's quite a bit of discomfort associated with having their permanent teeth begin to surface.

Chewing on your arms or feet is the equivalent of a person being a compulsive gum chewer. It's almost a reflex action. Since that's the case, your reaction to this should be very sudden and disturbing as well. The first thing you have to do is stand up abruptly if you're sitting or lying down with your puppy, then rewarding them if they don't follow you. Don't remain in a position of weakness. If you're already standing, extend your knee, once again followed by a reward if the behavior ceases. If you're sitting in a chair, your elbow can replace the knee as your correction tool with a reward for giving

up the jumping. You can see the connection between biting and jumping.

Jumping is what happens when they're no longer in a position to bite the part of your body they wish to bite. They normally target your feet and hands. If they bite your fingers, make a fist. In these situations, I would use a food reward after their correction as praising them by hand will make you an immediate target again. However, if you prefer not using a food reward, then offering them their favorite toy will suffice.

There are times, however, when neither of these corrections will work. Plan B is to try taking the part of your body they like to chew and spread something nontoxic but repulsive like vinegar on it. You can also pick up a safe solution like "Bitter Apple" at your local pet store. If you have a better home remedy, by all mean use it as long as it's safe. The way I learned to train never included the option of dominating a dog to smother bad behavior. I simply ignore the bad behavior until it becomes good, then I reward it. It leaves the dog with the feeling that he or she chose to behave well, leaving them feeling empowered. Puppies are such delicate creatures as are some adult dogs and building their self-confidence is always important. I once heard Dr. Laura Schlessinger say that the only way a person gains self-esteem is to do something they didn't believe they could do, therefore impressing themselves. It's no different for dogs, old and young.

JUMPING ON VISITORS AT THE DOOR

There are a couple of ways to eliminate the problem of your dog greeting visitors too enthusiastically. Both ways require that the dog be wearing their short leash and collar.

The first way is to have the dog on leash and correct them by gently pulling them back when they attempt to jump up on someone. You will answer the door with leash in one hand—and wait for the dog to attempt jumping up. If they jump up, pull them down and reward them. The visitor should pay no attention to the dog. The more your guest ignores your canine companion, the sooner your dog will become disinterested.

If the dog doesn't attempt jumping, you'll also reward them. We're simply bridging that moment of good behavior with praise and/or a goody. It's important to balance correction with affection so as not to emphasize the negative behavior exhibited by your dog. This is motivational in that it emphasizes the good and minimizes the bad. If you put too much emphasis on what the dog is doing wrong, they often will try doing it more. Training is often about reverse psychology; making the dog believe they enjoy something when they don't, as well as making it appear that their bad behavior doesn't bother you at all.

Since the doorbell is often the stimulus for bad behavior, I'll sometimes ask a friend or family member to rehearse knocking on the door or ringing the doorbell prior to an actual guest appearing. Then that appointed person would simulate being a visitor and be invited into the house. If the dog attempts to jump on your appointed guinea pig, have them correct the dog by turning a hip or extending a knee. This will force the dog down where he or she can be rewarded. Both you *and* your simulated houseguest will reward them. The praise will

be offered low so the dog doesn't have to come up for the praise, thus undoing their good behavior. Only reward when the dog is in the position you desire.

The other way to curtail jumping involves using a distraction tool. It can be a favorite toy or something they fear; it just has to be capable of getting their attention. When the dog jumps on your guest or simulated guest, throw your distraction object from behind. It's important that they not see you throw the object as to imply it comes from a "higher power" and not from you. Make sure you throw it close enough for your dog to notice it. Dogs assume you're innocent unless proven guilty. They will not take this distraction personally. This method may not always work, but it's certainly an option. Once again if the distraction tool stops the jumping, then they must be rewarded immediately. If they begin jumping again, use the attached short leash to correct them as the distraction tool can only be used from behind and at a distance.

CHEWING OBJECTS AND JUMPING ON OTHER PEOPLE

I've never seen a puppy who doesn't like to run and jump and play, assuming they're healthy. Their idea of play, however, can begin to morph into something with which you're not very pleased. It can develop into playing with objects that aren't their toys, chewing on furniture, or jumping on anyone who moves. This is why we will first introduce a short leash and slip collar to the equation. You can also use a leash converted to a slip leash (see illustration). Considering the puppy hasn't been restricted by any leash up to this point, simply putting the leash and collar on will disrupt their rebellious pattern. They may even take out their frustrations on the leash itself. This is all to be expected and welcomed. It would be preferable that you have to buy a new leash than new furniture or new shoes.

We're not making the puppy stop chewing, we're simply redirecting their focus from a restricted target, whatever that may be. Getting used to the leash now will also make it easier to walk the dog when

the time comes. From day one, the leash will signify work. Play will never involve having a leash or training collar on. Just make it clear to yourself and the dog which situation exists at any given moment. The presence of the leash and collar would mean good behavior is expected until it's removed.

When your puppy has gotten accustomed to wearing the training tools, they may begin to ignore this fact and go back to chewing or jumping on someone. This is when you would begin carrying a small throw-chain as your distraction tool. If the pup goes after someone other than you—or something like shoes or furniture—this is the time to be prepared. The best correction occurs when the bad behavior begins, not after the fact.

When your puppy cannot see you and is engaging in bad behavior, toss the chain toward the dog, the target being their rear feet. When the puppy turns to see what just landed, you can praise them right away. They will probably have forgotten what bad thing they were doing before you threw the chain. Then you simply wait for it to occur again. It's okay to use hand praise when they're going after someone else, just not when you yourself are the target. Hands should always be used for praise; never for correction. After you've used the chain correction a few times—accurately—they will begin to disengage from the offensive act upon simply hearing the jingle of the chain. That's when you're in the driver's seat as trainer.

Toys can be thrown toward the dog as an alternative, though they aren't normally as effective as the resulting *thump* is not as pronounced. You can make contact with the dog as long as it doesn't endanger him or her. You have to get their attention; if you miss their hind end and the object lands on a muted surface, their bad behavior probably won't stop. I can't stress enough how important it is to reward them immediately after the bad behavior comes to a halt.

The best position to monitor any dog's behavior is standing directly behind them where they cannot prove where the distraction tool originated. Whether we're talking about an adult dog or a puppy, you'll always have the most power where the dog can't see you. Most dogs find it difficult to focus on something in front of them as well as your correction from behind. Assuming the leash and collar are always on in every training situation, you will always have something to grab if needed, rather than the dog. The distraction tool is multipurpose. It can be used for any bad behavior like barking, digging, recall; you name it. The tool's greatest effect is one of surprise. Remember, the dog should never see you throw it. They will not connect you with the correction this way and will have to pay more attention to the sound of the chain whenever they hear it. Even if they know you have the throw-chain, they won't hold it against you. This is why you can jingle it for attention whether or not you intend to throw it. It's the not knowing part that keeps them tuned in.

YOUR DOG'S TRIGGERS

Much of getting to know your dog is to understand what can trigger their bad behavior. Let's say you're walking your dog "short" on his or her long leash and you run across a dog ferociously barking at you two from across the street, and your dog barks back. Keep in mind that most aggression is really fear in disguise. The way to determine if your dog is exhibiting "fear aggression" is to set a boundary like the curb for them. Then go in the opposite direction toward the end of your leash while making sure they don't go beyond that curb—simply climb the leash until you're holding the handle. If they run back toward you when you retreat, then their aggression is fear-based.

Aggression that's not fear-based would be seen in the dog that doesn't retreat. In this case you would call them back to you. They will be rewarded heavily for returning to you whether you reeled them in or they came out of fear. This scenario is an opportunity to work on your "recall" under duress.

A lot of pet owners believe that comforting their dog will make them feel more secure. Any situation where the dog is touched by hand while exhibiting bad behavior is tantamount to praising that undesired behavior and validating any fear they may have.

If I'm working with a dog exhibiting bad behavior, I want to put the dog on their own "island" by building separation from me. It's like that drunk guy in the bar who starts a fight with another guy—his friends are holding him back, but that's what he's counting on. If nobody was there, he'd have no protection and would probably just go back to quietly drinking his beer. He would know that he's on his own in this fight, that nobody is going to come to his rescue.

This is exactly how your dog sees the situation when you're retreating from the situation, that no aid will be coming from you.

It's important to recognize how close contact to your body can empower your dog to pick a fight they don't really want. Your dog should only be allowed to be close to you when their behavior is good.

The attitude you take is to ignore bad behavior and walk away like a parent from a kid protesting leaving Chuck E. Cheese. Remember that the worst punishment you can give your dog is to ignore them or their concerns. Punishment, if done by hand, can often be perceived as praise or at the very least it is attention.

This is just the beginning of your journey to understanding your dog and what propels some of their bad behavior. Being consistent with your training—at *least* fifteen minutes a day—can maintain good behavior. It's also good for you, the trainer, to give the dogs breaks during multiple training sessions.

Each session should be no more than fifteen to twenty minutes—with a short recess in between—much like a school kindergarten class. Dogs, like small children, need an intermittent recharge.

It's also good to end each session on a high note, not when the dog is performing poorly or is mentally or physically fatigued. Dogs tend to remember the last part of your session, whether it's one in the morning or two in the afternoon. Make the end of your training sessions memorable with the dog wanting more.

CHAPTER SEVEN

THE THREE ESSENTIALS TO EFFECTIVE TRAINING: EXPOSURE, DISTANCE, AND DURATION

Never discount the power of a dog's personality. It's the core of what makes a dog "your" dog. Training a dog should never change their identity. The dog training experience I gained from growing up around some exceptional, world-renowned dog trainers looms large in my life. It's given me a foundation that allows me to recognize the weaknesses and strengths in each dog I now encounter in my private training practice. I've learned that a dog's weakness can be converted into a strength with the right training.

I have seen almost every dog scenario you can imagine. I've been attacked by dogs on film and have separated random dog fights on the street. I've seen the good and the bad; the expected and the unexpected.

The hefty sample size of my own exposure to training means I'm not really surprised by anything when it comes to dogs. I can usually walk a dog down the street and learn everything I need to know about him or her by sheer observation. Some dogs reveal themselves as soon as I walk into their house. This only confirms to me that every dog is unique and the approach to training each one must be tailored to the individual dog. And the training must evolve organically. Watch your dog's tendencies as you train. His or her reaction to training tells you a lot about what kind of dog you're dealing with.

We can't just take the leash off one dog and place it on another with the same strategy in mind. The dog's disposition will reveal itself immediately after putting on their leash. Are they fearful and timid or are they anxious and wild? The amount of force needed for any particular dog is merely to counter any resistance they're offering to the training process. We never initiate force. Corrections can be either verbal or physical. The correction one dog absorbs comfortably can crush the spirit of another.

Karl Miller, whom I assisted on such movies as *Beethoven* and *K-9*, always said that a trainer needs to "balance correction with affection." This simply means that if your praise is bland, then your correction must be equally bland. By the same token, if your praise is strong, then your correction must be proportionately as strong. It's like an emotional teeter-totter. The focus a dog maintains is when the positive and the negative stimulus are balanced. Too much praise can make a dog lose focus while not enough can make them lose interest. Any force you end up using as a correction will be supplied by the dog's momentum to avoid compliance. Some dogs are more responsive and don't require much energy to correct them, while others will test your resolve with regularity. All dogs want to establish their boundaries with you and will cross those boundaries so that you *will* correct them. Then they know what *not* to do. Consistency is the key. Whatever you want from your dog today should apply tomorrow. If it's right then it must be acknowledged along with the bad. Never emphasize a correction due to a dog's lack of understanding, only a lack of effort.

Focus isn't something a dog is born with. The focus a dog possesses comes from knowing your expectations in any given situation. It's the most important thing a movie dog can have. It comes from experience. Some dogs attain focus quickly while others take longer. A dog that demonstrates less focus doesn't need more force, just more repetition. The number of times a dog must repeat doing something in order to master it varies with each dog. My dad used to say, "When the dog does it perfect every time, that's when you don't have to teach it anymore." There are times when a dog just "gets it" based on their own natural strengths and weaknesses and other times when it takes longer for the training to click. Some dogs will learn a certain behavior very quickly; while others can be more challenging. It isn't a matter of intelligence, but rather one of aptitude.

A perfect example of this is when I trained basics on an Australian Shepherd named Ozzie. She learned all the basics I normally teach dogs: Stay, Come, and Heel. Then from there her owner and I discovered things Ozzie did naturally and added those to her basic repertoire. A relatively simple behavior like "Heel" took multiple lessons to teach her, yet I taught her to jump into her owner's arms in about twenty minutes. It wasn't because I'm some kind of amazing trainer—it was simply a skill that I felt could be taught to her easily since she had an obvious natural jumping ability. I've had dogs lying down during training who knew they couldn't get up and began crawling toward me instead. I would then turn that "bad" behavior into one I could tap into on command by saying "Crawl."

Many of my clients' dogs learned "speak" simply because I found a situation that caused them to bark naturally and so I put a cue on it. My father always said the best way to stop a dog from barking at nothing is to put a cue (command) on their barking. Then they begin to bark only when you ask for it, not just when they feel like it. The point of these examples is to illustrate that every dog has their own strengths and weaknesses. It's the owner who recognizes them and taps into those skills that gets the furthest with their dog.

GO DOGS AND STAY DOGS

There are basically two types of dogs I've dealt with all these years: The "go" dogs and the "stay" dogs. The "go" dogs are good at things requiring movement like jumping, running, and catching. They are the acrobatic dogs. They're the dogs that usually get bored quite easily—they typically pull when on a walk; they don't like staying in any one place for too long. These are the dogs where an emphasis on slowing them down is paramount. Making dogs like these wait for everything can teach them to be more patient. The strategy with these dogs is to not allow them momentum.

The "stay" dogs, on the other hand, tend to be more fearful and sensitive to verbal or physical correction. Since they're more sensitive, they tend to require a quieter correction voice and extremely mild physical corrections. These dogs also tend to require more verbal praise to get their motor going and begin building their confidence. They tend to pull less on walks and are generally less independent than the "go" dogs. They need to be sped up while the "go" dogs need to be slowed down. Knowing which kind of dog you have will give you a good idea of whether you need to amp up your praise or tone it down.

After you've assessed your dog's strengths and weaknesses, you can begin to build on that by exposing them to different situations (the same rule applies to puppies, assuming they've had their second round of immunizations).

THE IMPORTANCE OF EXPOSURE

What I refer to as "exposure" will be the base of your training pyramid. I spent much of my time in the film industry taking future movie dogs to shopping centers and feeding them dinner near bus stops or revolving doors. I took them to places where there were loud noises and a lot of activity. What other way could I simulate the chaos of being on a movie set without subjecting them to some uncertainty prior to going on their first shoot? These doses of exposure prepared them for the possibility of meeting other dogs, experiencing new sounds, or becoming familiar with crowds of people. Most importantly, it allowed me to discover any fears they might have sooner rather than later. The earlier we find the problem, the easier it is to fix. We simply simulate the things we want them to endure happily. For example, if a dog is afraid of loud noises, it's your responsibility as a pet owner to avoid insulating them from these noises. Ever heard of the phrase "what doesn't kill you makes you stronger"? This is relevant because rather than saving them from their fears, we will allow them to absorb the thing they fear in small doses at first and increasingly over time. If they're afraid of cars, let's say, the last thing we want to do is avoid cars. In fact, every time this dog sees a car, I would have a food reward ready before they react negatively. They may not eat that food if they're too frightened, but over time they'll take it. That's when you will know they're overcoming their fear.

Fear can express itself in the form or barking, cowering, pulling, or trying to escape the situation. The barking dog might appear aggressive at first but its reaction is normally just due to a lack of exposure. Dogs, like people, tend to fear that which they don't understand or that which is unfamiliar to them. Associating food with everything they fear will desensitize the dog to that fear over time. Facing your dog's fears head on without reservation is always preferable to trying to protect the dog from them. The only time you should protect your dog is if they are in physical danger; not simply because they're uncomfortable.

How many times on the streets do I see an owner with a small dog who reacts negatively to any dog they encounter? The owner of this yapping dog will either scold their dog or pick it up and retreat back to the safety of their home. The impression given to the dog by the owner is that fear is bad (scolding) or that this behavior is great (being picked up).

We may think we're sending one message to our dog when we're sending a completely different one. That's why I always recommend not making any physical contact with your dog when they're in a condition of distress for any reason. The best way to deal with a dog's fear is not to acknowledge it, or at least minimize your reaction to it. Any contact or verbal reaction on your part will justify their fears. Getting my canine student exposure is the very first thing I would do before I begin to teach them anything substantial. A calm dog will be a faster learner since routine distractions will soon be ignored and looked upon as normal.

THE POWER OF DISTANCE

I've touched briefly on the power of distance when it comes to training your dog. Much like exposure, distance is extremely important when working with dogs in film since there isn't really anywhere for the dog trainer to be. How far you can be from the dog when teaching them "Stay" can also be vital in everyday life since you want to be able to enforce it without being right next to your dog.

How close do you need to be when your dog is on a "Stay"? There isn't any hard, fast rule regarding distance, but the farther the better. If you're only comfortable leaving your dog on a "Stay" from four feet, then that, too, is okay. It will serve as a base from which to expand that distance. Extending the distance between you and your dog will come in increments.

Another distance-related behavior is something commonly referred to as "the recall." How far away can your dog be from you and still obey the command to "Come"? It's a viable question since it can be the difference between life and death for your canine companion. After a car has to slam on their brakes—or worse—isn't the time to address your dog's shortcomings in this area. "Stay" and "Come" are the two single most important training issues to address. They come before anything else. Whatever time you can allot for training your dog needs to be primarily devoted to these two commands. Every trick you end up teaching your dog is built upon these foundation behaviors. A dog that reliably returns to you will give you the confidence to stretch the distance for "Stay" because you'll be safe in the knowledge that you can simply start over from their original location. A recall that's dependable will serve as a backup to any shortcoming they may have in other areas of their training. Look at it like a parachute when the plane is going down. You'll find you can't anticipate what bizarre things may happen when you're with your dog and often a recall will bail you out of an unexpected occurrence. Being next to you should be looked upon as a safe place no matter how long it takes your dog to come to you. Obviously, there isn't any punishment to be given upon their arrival, lest they hesitate on your next recall. If they do hesitate on their next recall, simply reel them in with the long leash more vigorously and reward.

Now that we've discussed exposure and distance, there is one more basic element to consider. I will refer to it as "duration" for lack of a fancier word.

DURATION

Duration refers to the amount of time a dog can continue performing a behavior without needing a break. There's a reason why kindergarten children are given a periodic recess during class. It's simply because young brains need regular breaks in order to take on more information. A dog's cerebral peak seldom goes very far beyond that of a four-year-old child. Keeping this in mind, I never work my canine students beyond fifteen minutes at a time in the early part of their training. I find they lose focus when working on something too long. I've also found that every mini session should end on a high note as dogs and children tend to remember what happened at the end of their lessons, opposed to the beginning. By the same token, the lesson that ends on a negative will carry over to the next lesson. It's like riding a roller coaster. It's scary facing it, then after you're done, you want to do it again.

We always want to leave our dog with that positive feeling that comes from doing something they were uncertain about in the beginning. Then you'll notice as your dog's education broadens, they'll be able to perform for longer segments of time. Your dog will be able to stay longer due to the exposure they've received as their confidence will filter out most distractions. Depending on the type of dog you have—a "stay" dog or a "go" dog—you may extend certain types of sessions. For example, the "stay" dog may be able to stay for a long time but may tire performing actions such as coming, jumping, and retrieving. The "go" dog can run all day but find staying in one place much more challenging. The bottom line is that the fifteen-minute rule can be lengthened if what the dog is doing doesn't really seem like work to them. We aren't a lot different from our dogs as we tend to see time fly when we're enjoying what we're doing. Just keep in mind there will be some behaviors that are more challenging for some dogs than others. This is why knowing your dog's limitations early will pay dividends down the road.

CHAPTER EIGHT

STRESS AND DECOMPRESSION AND THEIR ROLE IN BEHAVIOR MODIFICATION

I can safely say as human beings we've all been stressed, even overwhelmed, by the enormity of certain events in our lives. Not only have I had that feeling of being on edge, I've also observed that feeling manifesting with my fellow humans. Stress can come in many forms. It can appear as a muted panic. It can also appear in the form of tunnel vision leading to carelessness and dumb mistakes. It can lead us to sweat and breathe heavily. There are all kinds of subtle ways in which we can display our uneasiness.

Early in my movie dog training career, I moonlighted a bit as an actor. While my acting skills were somewhat one-dimensional, I can honestly say that I've been on quite a few auditions, normally reading for some type of villain role. Prior to reading in front of a casting director, the competing actors are typically given "sides"—a page of dialogue that features lines of the character they yearn to portray. Once called in, the casting director will typically read the lines of the other character engaged in this page of conversation.

Prior to the big reading, actors are bundled together in another room awaiting their opportunity. Each actor is in their own world going over lines in their head. While every actor may rehearse to themselves a little differently, there's one thing I've always noticed: Many of them were every bit as nervous as I was. Sometimes tension revealed itself in the form of pacing or biting nails. Sometimes the actors would break out in a sweat or fidget with themselves. Then there were those actors who simply would break out into a series of yawns.

When we see a person yawning, we just assume the person didn't get enough sleep. The same could be said of our canine best friend. They're just tired, right? Wrong!

Dogs—like people—often show stress in similar ways. One common emotional outlet is when each begins a pattern of yawning as they deal with the uncertainty of a stressful situation.

The reason is simple. The anticipation of an upcoming event can lead us—and our dogs—to breathe heavier. It's like a low-grade form of hyperventilation. When we hyperventilate, we begin to swallow oxygen instead of breathing it. This builds up and is regurgitated in the form of a yawn. The act of yawning can often be like letting air out of a helium balloon. It normally has the effect of releasing a bit of tension each time it is repeated.

Just as yawns rarely symbolize grogginess, panting in a dog doesn't always represent being overheated. Each behavior—when occurring in dogs—can mean something completely different.

EXPOSURE AND DECOMPRESSION

I train many dogs with various forms of anxiety. I strongly believe in facing fears. While there are many owners who think they're helping their dog by removing them from uncomfortable situations, I know it's a poor long-term solution. It may be convenient at the time but it will only feed the fear. The only way to get a dog over something they fear is to give them no exit strategy from that situation. This means that if we see another dog, a trash truck, or the mailman, we have to teach our best friend to endure the discomfort.

While you may think you're doing your dog a favor insulating them from frightening things, you're actually inhibiting their emotional development. You're hindering their ability to grow and accept. Removing your dog from difficult situations teaches him or her that they can always expect to be saved from anything uncomfortable. You're setting a pattern they learn to exploit.

Since I've become more of a dog behaviorist than dog trainer in recent years, I know that improvement in a dog's self-esteem comes in stages. The dog that runs away must be slowed before they can be stopped. The dog that's aggressive must be calmed before they can be quieted. It's all about keeping realistic goals and making daily incremental progress. Dog training isn't about hitting home runs every time you're at bat, it's about consistent contact. In this case, once again, we're talking about the importance of exposure.

Exposure to new things can result in chaos for anxious dogs. Exposure isn't just about geographical locations; it's about what that location means to your best friend. It's all about reforming memories. Location doesn't matter—it only matters what that location represents to your dog.

Through experience I've learned that exposure is about the elements—and I'm not referring to the weather. The elements I'm speaking of are people, animals, and things. When you keep your laundry list short and simple, it's much easier to conquer.

Regardless of what your dog's particular fear may be, the antidote is often quite similar. It's all about boundaries—geographical boundaries. If your dog has difficulty exercising restraint in the presence of specific distractions, the key is "putting them in the stands." This means your dog should have a front row seat to view whatever it is that makes them anxious.

The boundary could be the curb as your dog's trigger passes on the other side. It could be the grass adjoining a parking lot where other dogs disembark. It could be the living room rug while the family is eating. Basically, you're setting broad and clear boundaries with obvious distractions. It doesn't matter whether your dog sits or lies down, it only matters that they respect the physical limits you've set. Then when situations change you may augment those boundaries. They can constantly change but only with your express permission. When I use the command "Okay," it means that those boundaries disappear until reinstalled.

While a dog who's agitated may pull on your leash or bark, typically it doesn't mean your dog wants to fight. Often it means they want to scare the offending distraction or prompt you to protect them. If the other dog or the mailman is the offensive presence, it's your reaction—or lack of it—that can dictate your best friend's behavior.

The thought process to a dog that has a boundary is that they begin to feel protected over time by that boundary. It begins to become an imaginary wall. As the dog realizes they can't get *to* the distraction they will begin to believe that it somehow protects them *from* that distraction. The reaction I have when my dog misbehaves is one of firm indifference. I'm telling my best friend, "I see what you see but it means nothing to me." I'm not too close to my dog when they're agitated; only when the agitation subsides. That's when the praise begins. Never comfort the bad behavior, wait for silence or calmness and reward *that* behavior. There's no sense in reprimanding bad behavior if you're not going to recognize its subsequent disappearance. When a dog misbehaves, I act as if they just passed gas. I move away but I'm maintaining the designated boundary.

Typically, when our dog's barking begins to fade, so will their pulling—and vice versa. We've taken away the thrust of their anxiety. Those two reactions seem to go hand in hand and dissipate in sequence or in tandem. Then when your best friend is calmly watching distractions from their boundary, the last bit of "decompression" begins. Anxiety doesn't disappear all at once, but in stages. I compare it to letting air out of a balloon without letting the balloon fly away. The goal of this process is for the dog to share our indifference to that other dog, blowing flag, or motorcycle—whatever it may be.

As a dog trainer I reward when teaching new parlor tricks, but I reward even more in anxiety suppression training. I prefer emphasizing the good reaction more than reprimanding the bad reaction.

Each time your dog shows calmness in the face of perceived danger, they should get food and praise. The idea is to reprogram the way your dog perceives danger. I like to think that my canine student will begin to think they will be "paid" every time danger arrives. It's the act of changing expectations. It's pure and simple reconditioning.

Once your dog is staying well and calm in a large area, you can make the stay in the face of distraction more specific. While your dog may have initially stayed on the curb, we may next move them to a more specific mark like a sidewalk grate or small patch of grass. It's only then when we should begin seeking perfection when giving a specific command like "Sit" or "Lie down." Remember to fix the unseemly overall behavior before you begin attempts to dazzle guests with "tricks." Less is more; a dog that you don't notice is the best dog of all.

Now that your new mark allows for less movement, you'll begin to see the final signs of decompression. Let's say first the pulling stopped, then the barking. Let's go even further and say that the barking then evolved into a whine. Each new stage represents a greater level of canine calmness. The final stage can involve one of two subtle canine behaviors.

My grandfather and my father were rather obsessed about dogs taking care of all their business before arriving on a movie set. When Lassie was handed over to Rudd or my father, the first question they asked was, "Did they poop?" Normally Lassie either had gone or the trainer would tell them he didn't need to go. Once in a while, an assistant would reply "He went" even if they knew he didn't. Whether they were lying or not, my predecessors would always know because of one simple sign: the dog was panting. A dog that's panting and properly hydrated on a cool day can only mean one thing.

While panting can obviously mean a dog is hot or thirsty, we now know it can mean a bathroom break is urgently needed. It can also be a sign that a dog is healing emotionally. It happens in concert with air being swallowed through panting (heavy breathing). It's the final stage of a dog exercising restraint from engaging in behavior they once could not resist. This mild resistance is the "new" normal. When the panting evaporates, the yawning will begin.

When I first begin working with a dog owner, "Stay" is at the top of every wish list. When I say stay it means "Stay" in the midst of distractions. It could be activity by family members or strangers on the street. Some dogs take to "Stay" like ducks take to water, but the "go dogs" tend to struggle more with it. When they're first asked to stay on a mark, they will make at least a few escape attempts. We will welcome that in training. Every time you catch them and use the leash to take them back, it accelerates the learning process.

Then when they're beginning to catch on to the mark, the escape attempts will evaporate. Then you'll see your dog pant and then yawn. This is a good sign. This reaction tells me that our best friend is releasing that last bit of tension. What began as ferocious barking or light urination is now merely a yawn. When the yawning wears itself out, that's when you know you're at the finish line on that behavior.

A very good test is having your dog stay on any area close to where eating takes place. If your dog can stay on a nearby rug for the duration of a family meal, you have a solid stay. You want to make sure that when you finally give the dog the "Okay," they receive a special bonus. I prefer it be something they don't normally receive, within reason. If they were paid in silver normally, now it's time to pay in gold bullion.

Every time your dog is forced to ignore distractions when working goes toward developing a well-rounded dog. This applies to walking by your side and recall. Anyone can get their dog to perform when the situation is static, but it's all about gradually raising the degree of difficulty. I know that from growing up in Hollywood and working with my own dogs on a movie set. I learned early on that working dogs on a movie set is a true ten when it comes to the degree of difficulty.

When a dog is first faced with something unfamiliar they become tense, unable to relax. They're standing as if about to take off at any time. Sometimes hackles are raised, even if they aren't barking or whining. Allowing that tension to deflate is much more effective than forcing it out of them. This is the reason I practice the "mark" in this situation freestyle. Auto sit will suppress the behavior temporarily, but it won't allow calmness to happen organically. It's merely a smoke screen. I believe the same is true when applying pain-inducing alternatives like shock collars.

A dog that decompresses naturally will choose to sit or lie down after all their noises, tension, and yawning subside. It's very rare to see a dog yawning that's already lying down—unless they've just woken up.

The use of a long leash is a great barometer of a dog's tension as well. If they're pulling and you're using a short leash, decompression cannot occur without force. I'm never pulling a dog away from something they want; I'm merely using their own freedom against them. I never have to hold them back, I just let them run into their own correction. They end up feeling that they've corrected themselves rather than looking at us as the reason they're not free. Sometimes they take it out on the leash itself.

This is why correction can never occur through the hands. I can't emphasize enough the importance of playing that poker game with your dog. Dogs are always watching our face and our hands. If our face doesn't show emotion and our hands aren't used to display force, we never personalize our corrections. Shoving their rear end with a foot when they feel tension is much more effective than lifting their front end off the ground by the leash, as I observe many trainers doing.

If you encounter anxiety with your dog and you don't have the luxury of separating yourself from the dog and their boundary, using your body is the best option. Let's say you're with your dog and they become agitated by another dog, person, or thing. Let's also imagine that you aren't across the street from the distraction already. Let's say they're approaching on your side of the street. While we don't want to confront the distraction, necessarily we want to stay within range. We never want our dog to get the impression we're retreating as that would only serve to confirm their fears.

Whether it's another dog or a kid on a bike—whatever it is that agitates them—we just want to find a place to be while they pass. If they're passing on a sidewalk we could use a driveway or a patch of grass as our boundary. Then we can use our body to shove our dog rather than relying on the leash alone. We want our focus to be on the boundary, not the distraction. The key is not using our hands and keeping our dog in front of us. The voice should be firm. You want to convey the feeling that your dog's behavior is simply ridiculous and that the situation doesn't warrant the behavior. If you touch your dog when they're under duress, they will typically reignite, and decompression cannot occur. The same rule applies to comforting baby talk. Remember, actions speak louder than words. I reserve words for important things as too many words can make each one less effective.

Decompression is a huge part of behavior modification. Decompression is when your dog's exclamation point merely becomes a period. It's when a yell becomes a whisper. It's the end result to getting two dogs to coexist in the same household. It's when you know that your dog is finally accepting the new cat.

Decompression is the goal of all that exposure. You will know when it has occurred. You won't only notice it occurring but it should also bring a feeling of accomplishment. Dog training is a lot more than getting a dog to do what you want. It's also about feeling good when it's accomplished. Mental scars left from harsh training techniques can manifest into something even worse down the road. If freedom is what a dog wants, then good behavior is how they achieve that objective.

Hopefully by now you know the underlying theme of my training. It's never been about force. It's about giving a dog options and allowing them to make the right choice. There are many harsh training options out there. They're seldom taught because it's good for the dog, but rather because they're easy for the owner.

I realize some of my techniques will take some time to master. It's like driving a car. The reason it may seem a bit more complicated is because it's not designed for simplicity, it's designed for canine development. There are no side effects to training when done with consistency and kindness.

Decompression is like using a slow cooker instead of a microwave. The microwave will get the job done quickly, but it will taste a bit different. I never want you to taste the flavor of expediency. It's about quality over quantity. I'd rather have one great trained dog than three poorly trained ones.

Growing up watching my father and grandfather train all these marvelous tricks was an amazing experience—it was like a magic show. However, as I got older, I realized that the greatest trick they taught wasn't quite so obvious. They simply made great dogs. The training of Lassie came easy because making the dog came before training him.

You may not be able to control every poorly behaved dog you encounter. There will be surprises—you should expect that. The only thing you should expect is your own dog's good behavior. This is true because they've been tested by fire. You haven't sheltered your best friend and you've never raised your hand to them. That's how you get to the pinnacle of dog ownership. Once your dog has climbed Mount Everest, Mount Fuji will seem like a mere speed bump. Everything in the future is relative to what you've endured in the past. This goes for your dog as well.

CHAPTER NINE

YOUR DOG AND ANXIETY

As I've said more than once, every dog is different; no two are exactly alike. In keeping with that, most dog owners may at some point experience some unexpected canine problems. Because I've talked to so many dog owners, I want to share some information about a major root cause of many canine behavioral problems: anxiety.

SEPARATION ANXIETY–ITS PREVENTION AND CURE

Anxiety comes in different forms, but for many dogs, the most pressing is Separation Anxiety. It can reveal itself in very subtle ways or very disturbing ways. Sometimes the problem is one the new owner has inherited; other times it's a situation the new owner has created. The causes are numerous. One thing I know for certain: Dogs aren't born with the condition. It isn't inherited like hip dysplasia or epilepsy. The roots are often environmental, much like the majority of canine behavioral issues.

Tracing the path of Separation Anxiety can take us all the way back to the breeder and how those dogs were handled as puppies. The root may also be connected to one or more traumatic events that happened under your ownership, even if you never witnessed or recognized the triggering event.

It's a malady that's difficult to measure by comparing it with that of other dogs. This is because each dog's present environment is unique, as is their past experience. Since all dogs are individuals, each one will exhibit anxiety in a different manner. Some will bark, some will become destructive, and others will attempt escape.

Since we can't go back and erase events or situations that existed before you owned the dog, we have to concentrate on fixing what you're witnessing today. The key to acquiring canine security is in creating structure and consistency in your dog's routine from day one. Many of the dogs who are anxious normally have very good reason to be. Much of their uncertainty comes from simply not knowing where they're going to be living tomorrow. Repeated relocation is very common with many dogs, particularly those coming from shelters. Dogs that have had more than one home typically comprise the largest percentage of anxious dogs. Consistency is something these dogs have never enjoyed. However, it's easier to fix this with puppies than with adult dogs.

Regardless of a dog's unstable past, we can only concern ourselves with their future under our ownership. Is our dog enveloped in a feeling of stability and security in our home? Do we have a long-term plan for the care of our dog? Are we giving our new family member a feeling of predictability and comfort? It's all about expectations. Your dog's reality begins to be established in your home the day they arrive. Having seen firsthand the way different owners handle new dog ownership, I'll illustrate the importance of basic structure by using two fictional dog owners.

Owner A

Dog Owner A knows what they want from their dog right out of the gate. The rules set by this dog owner are clearly defined from day one. This owner already envisions and implements a clear routine for their dog before the dog enters their new home. They've already determined what behavior will be tolerated from their dog or puppy and won't allow those rules to be compromised.

This owner doesn't establish one set of rules only to change them later. They determine where the dog will sleep, for example, and never alter that location without a very good reason. They don't spoil their dogs upon arrival, only to tighten the rules later.

One example of spoiling dogs would be allowing a puppy to sleep in your bed only to prohibit it later when they become too big. It's unfair to give too much freedom to a dog only to take it away when it becomes inconvenient. Dogs quickly detect patterns in our routine soon after entering any unfamiliar environment. For this reason, we should never confuse our dog with inconsistent rules.

Owner A also crate trains their dog from day one and does so responsibly, as depicted in Chapter Three. Their dog has been trained to see the crate as a safe place, a refuge, not a prison.

Owner B

Then there's Dog Owner B. They aren't quite as well prepared for dog ownership as Dog Owner A. They're basically just winging it. They allow their new dog to get away with anything. Maybe they're preoccupied or busy with other things. Possibly they just don't enforce any of their canine rules, assuming canine boundaries actually ever existed in the first place.

If they do use the crate, they typically use it only for punishment. Going into the crate is normally accompanied by an angry voice or physical reprimand. They're painting their dog's potential sanctuary as a prison cell. They're not providing the positive meaning we want the crate to represent.

Owner B lets emotion guide their dog ownership experience. They reveal everything in their voice and their body language. They're not consistent in raising their dog; it's all based on their mood at that particular day or moment. They don't typically balance correction with affection. Owner B often emphasizes a dog's faults instead of his or her achievements.

The unprepared dog owner will not be thinking ahead. They won't be considering how the dog interprets putting on a coat or grabbing car keys. They often won't acquire a crate for their dog until the dog has already had a separation anxiety incident. They don't have a plan like Dog Owner A does.

One cause of separation anxiety can be if you leave for vacation and can't take your dog with you. I'm often asked the best options for leaving a dog while on vacation. I believe boarding, hiring a pet sitter, or leaving them at a friend's or family member's house can all be great options. The key to their happiness in your absence is having someone in the family circle care for them. If not a family member, then anyone with whom the dog is already familiar. I wouldn't recommend taking them to any kennel for boarding unless someone there is familiar to them upon arrival. Think of it: first *you* leave, then they're left to deal with strangers (and other dogs). That's a lot to take for many dogs. If your choice is leaving a dog with a friend, make sure any pets living with that person are familiar with your dog before entering their home.

The Cure for Separation Anxiety

Now that we've discussed the principles involved in Separation Anxiety prevention, how do we fix the Separation Anxiety that's inherited? What do we do if our dog goes crazy when we first attempt putting them into the crate? If we've acquired a previously owned dog, we don't always know what experiences the dog has had in a crate. Experience tells me the dog that vigorously opposes being in the crate has already had a negative experience with confinement. Possibly all those things Dog Owner B did or didn't do left a lasting impression on our new dog. Now we're paying the price.

There are three ways a dog will reject being left alone: They will bark, they will destroy things, or they will try to escape. The aftermath of such behavior will look a lot like rebellion but it isn't—it's just fear.

There are many trainers who will inflict pain on a dog who resists confinement. They will either physically correct the dog or use a shock collar. The reason I don't use these methods is because I know fear is already the catalyst. Why would I use pain in order to eliminate fear? It seems irrational. Let's look at how we can take on each symptom of confinement resistance.

BARKING

This is the most common way a dog expresses displeasure, and not just for being confined. This is why so many dogs locked in backyards bark as much as they do. In order for a dog to bark they must move; very seldom is barking not accompanied by movement of some sort.

Assuming your dog has already been subjected to some sort of acclimation to the crate, our job should be easy. The only difference between basic crate training and separation anxiety suppression is whether we're leaving or not. A dog that's not equipped to handle freedom in your home must have confinement bestowed upon them. Freedom is something a dog must earn; it isn't a canine birthright. This isn't to say that he or she will always be confined, but it's a good starting point. Leaving a dog loose at home with Separation Anxiety puts not only your furniture in jeopardy, but the dog as well. The dog could hurt themselves if they are triggered while alone and go into a panic mode.

I remind my clients how much dogs hate silence. I typically recommend a TV or radio be left on for our lonely, anxious dog. The white noise created not only keeps them company, but it also blocks out all the little peripheral noises they may hear while left alone. This includes car doors opening and closing, people yelling, or other car noises. Dogs hear everything, so we must attempt to mute their hearing to specific outside noises. A ticking clock can also bring comfort to our confined canine, giving them a feeling of being kept company. Many times, even covering their crate with a blanket or furniture pad will make the room surrounding their crate seem less ominous, as it will limit what they see and hear.

If your dog barks when left at home, correct the problem there before doing the same in the car, assuming it's cool enough for them to be left there. Certainly if your dog feels insecure at home, the chances are slim that they would feel more secure in your car away from home.

The best way to limit movement and squelch barking while crated is to make sure the crate isn't too big. It should be big enough for them to enter and turn around, but not too cavernous to impede their feeling of security. If all the things I've mentioned don't stop your dog from barking, there are a couple more backup plans available.

One plan is merely pretending you're leaving and hiding within earshot. If you hear barking, rush in like your hair is on fire and give them a verbal correction. If that makes them stop, make sure that a goody is given to them the moment the barking stops. Then "rinse and repeat." Setting the trap over and over will make your dog unsure if you're really leaving. It's all part of the Poker game we play with our dog.

If this plan doesn't solve the issue, I would hang a distraction, normally a chain collar, from the top of the crate. Placement is crucial as the chain should be placed near where the dog will end up barking; typically the corner of the crate closest to the door from where you exited. Since movement is normally required for a dog to bark, running into the chain will break their momentum and typically stop all barking.

The barking will eventually turn to whining before it disappears completely. Remember that repetition is the key. Never forget that the crate will be where they eat and where their toys will be kept.

Also remember there's no anger combined with confinement. It's a place to cool off, not a torture chamber. Remember to strategically place goodies in the crate when they aren't looking, giving them the illusion that good things *grow* in the crate.

DESTRUCTION

When a dog becomes destructive in your absence, whether loose or in the crate, it's a sign of fear. It may appear to be an act of rebellion, but it comes from a fearful place. If they can't handle being loose in the house due to their destruction, then you must move them to the crate in your absence. It's not cruel—it would be crueler to leave them to suffer through their fear of open spaces. Since I don't believe in inflicting pain through shocking devices, I must use a strong distraction to get a similar effect. The best course of action is to simulate leaving as we did for the barking dogs.

I think it's safe to say your claustrophobic dog will try to destroy their crate the moment we disappear from view. Since this behavior may not necessarily be accompanied by barking, we must put something in place that allows us to see when their destructive behavior begins. I recommend using one of those baby monitors with a camera.

These devices allow you to monitor the object's movements through a camera connected to your phone. Initially you may not need a camera as the destruction will begin immediately upon you exiting the home. Eventually the dog's bad behavior will take longer to emerge.

The moment bad behavior is detected, we will rush back inside as if the house is on fire. This act is not associated with anger, but chaos. I may even drop a distraction chain as I reenter. This will startle your dog and cause them to stop what they're doing long enough for you to toss a food reward into their crate.

Then you'll casually resume leaving the domain. We're just looking to extend the time they're able to stay confined. When they show real improvement, you can calmly reenter the home and release them from the crate. You will only release them on a high note, never because they're being bad. This act would clearly represent conceding to your dog's desires and/or fears. Remember food represents the bridge—that moment when good behavior is achieved.

ESCAPING

The philosophy is the same for a dog that tries to escape their confinement when you leave your home. Once again, we'll use the baby cam and reenter with urgency when the escape attempt begins. They will then respond to your entrance, at which time you'll bridge that achievement with a treat and leave again. Once again, try to refrain from any verbal praise as this will typically cause them to feel even more insecure. Remember, we want to make our exit a "throw away" moment; we don't want to attach any more emotion to it than already exists. We're only looking for incremental results initially, not complete success. Once a dog is able to endure confinement for around fifteen minutes, you're nearing completion of the process.

BALANCING AND REBALANCING THE HOUSEHOLD POWER STRUCTURE

Another form of anxiety for a dog occurs when a new human becomes part of the household. If you live alone and own a dog, it's not a daily necessity to bend to any other human's needs. You don't have to worry about what consequences you or your dog's behavior has on other individuals sharing your address. While some allowances can be made for guests, the everyday behavior of your dog primarily affects you. You alone decide how "good" dog behavior is defined in your residence.

As a trainer, I normally achieve the quickest results training dogs for single owners. There are fewer moving parts in the dog training process. Since I teach both owners *and* dogs, a maximum class size of just two students streamlines the sessions. Once I get the owner and their dog on the same page, my job is essentially done.

Down the road, things become more complicated as names on the residential mailbox grow. Whether you're adding a roommate, a spouse, and/or children, the power structure within the house will change almost immediately. While your dog has grown accustomed to you—and vice versa—how will they relate to your new household member? How will the newcomer relate to your dog?

Often the changing household dynamics aren't addressed until a problem emerges later. For this reason, we should anticipate any potential issues before they become reality. The dog and the new family member—or members—need to become well acquainted with each other before they begin sharing the same couch. We want to make sure the comfort zone extends equally in all directions.

Assuming your new human occupant feels comfortable with dogs, there are a couple of ways the acclimation process can go for your dog. Your canine companion can either embrace the new household dynamic, or can complicate it. Sometimes the dog can become protective of you; other times he or she just won't show the same respect toward your new housemate. Accordingly, you must give equal power to whoever moves in no matter how reluctant you are to relinquish that power.

The dog needs to know from day one that this new household member is also indispensable. This can be established through some simple bonding. The shortest route to a new bond can be established by the additional household member providing services that you normally provide—for instance, treats initially.

On our first meeting, I ask my clients who feeds the dog. I ask this because in a multiple-person household, it's the feeder that tends to be the biggest distraction during our training sessions. If there's a noticeable emotional imbalance, I will recommend that the roles be reversed. If the wife has been feeding the dog, then I recommend the husband take over that role. In cases like this, the person feeding may be reluctant to relinquish that role but I assure them that it's not permanent. We will only proceed this way until the imbalance has been rectified.

There's a common saying that a dog will never bite the hand that feeds it. While this is essentially true, the significance of walking a dog is often downplayed. I'm often amazed, even after all these years training, how the person who walks the dog is often looked upon even more fondly than the one who feeds them. You know by now my emphasis on the leash as a powerful behavior modification tool; it shouldn't just be the signal for a walk. If you're only using your leash for that purpose, then you're not taking full advantage of its influence.

There have been many times when training a new canine student where they're not eager to embrace a lot of new rules at first. This attitude changes shortly thereafter, normally when I take them on their first walk. Though *my* goal is to teach them obedience, the dog normally sees it as leading to something even more amazing. This is because so many of us only use that leash for walks. Now I already have the dog thinking of this positive result only with a different person and a different goal. I believe in keeping the dogs guessing as to our motives; it keeps them off-balance and allows us to maintain control.

The leash and training collar are so powerful that often any aggressive barking at a new individual can be quelled simply by the owner handing the leash to that person without the dog being given any commands. This can be accompanied by that person simultaneously dropping a favorite treat. The dog will see that as approval by their owner. In any case, the dog will look more fondly toward the person holding the leash. This is because of their connotation of what the leash represents: Walking/good times. Simply by that association, there's an expectation on the dog's part that overrides any initial hesitation.

While serving on board aircraft carriers in the Navy, there were many monotonous days intermixed with some exciting ones. The semiregular event sailors looked forward to the most was receiving mail. When you're out at sea for months at a time, you begin to appreciate the little things. You'd never expect that the mere prospect of getting a letter was enough to inspire such anticipation. It's the same for your dog and their walks.

Every time you walk your dog, it's just like a Navy mail call. It's something that can never be simulated in your own yard. While you might consider yourself a world traveler by going around the globe, your dog becomes one simply by going around the block.

A life spent in the backyard or in the house is like being at sea. Everything looks the same out there. You look one way and you see ocean; while the other direction you see more water. This brings us full circle to the term "exposure" explained in Chapter Seven. The more your dog experiences, the less surprised or tentative he or she will be in relation to any new experience. That transition doesn't happen in the backyard, no matter how much room it may have.

Both food and walking are job number-one as a pet owner. Walking a dog on a long leash will give you the option of the dog discovering things on their own without the owner standing over them. The connection you make with your dog "on leash" is crucial. If you're using your leash in a broad array of situations, there's no way for the dog to anticipate what's coming next. The one constant: there is always a positive result to any uncertain or taxing situation.

Once I begin training dogs for my clients, I recommend that the leash and training collar be used for any situation where good behavior is to be expected. This means the leash could signify not just a walk, but also a training session. It could also mean absolutely nothing. This is when you really gain the upper hand with your dog, as they're constantly off-balance guessing your next move. What does this leash mean? This is a much better scenario than your dog manipulating you to follow their agenda.

A Balanced Household

What does a balanced household look like? Let's look at an example of husband-and-wife dog owners who are expecting a baby. Just to add another element to the equation, let's envision grandma moving in prior to the baby's arrival. Our first goal in this scenario is to establish grandma's presence.

The day grandma arrives, the first thing we will have her do is feed your dog a treat immediately upon walking through the front door. If grandma is also physically fit enough to walk the dog, that would certainly be a bonus. When mealtime comes, she should be the one to put the bowl down for your canine best friend. Now your dog is already off-balance. Since grandma is feeding the dog, mom and dad don't become the focus and something to protect from this new person since they're no longer the sole oxygen source for your dog.

This simple adjustment in your dog's priorities will minimize the role of the household members your canine already loves and respects. The vacuum created by this move will create a more neutral feel to your dog's outlook toward each person in the household. This leads not only to an immediate love for grandma, but also a greater respect for her. It offsets the power the preexisting household members already possess. This will prove vital when grandma starts giving the dog simple commands like "Sit," "Stay," and "Come." However, the bond must be developed before commands are given.

We don't want grandma to be a spectator in your family dog training mission. We don't want our dog to take advantage of her in your absence. These bonding actions will give grandma confidence to handle the dog when nobody else is around. It will also relieve any anxiety the dog may have when being left with her or anyone else. The dog will be thinking, *I love mom and dad, but I can survive without them.* Separation anxiety is what happens when we place too much necessity on our presence alone.

How many times have we heard someone say, "My dog listens to so-and-so . . . he just doesn't listen to *me*"? It definitely doesn't have to be that way if we rebalance the household every time it tips the wrong way. Often the rebalancing may even begin to favor the newcomer. If this becomes the case, we will reclaim our previous role of sole provider. The weakest link at home should always become the provider of food and/or walks or anything that stimulates your dog. This keeps the teeter-totter level. Once things are level it's not a bad idea to split duties when possible, to maintain the new balance.

Now that grandma has been accepted, we must get our dog to accept a newborn baby. This very needy new household addition will be a threat to many established dogs. They're also the most vulnerable. Our best friend's role will certainly be challenged. The only way to get a dog to truly accept this helpless being is to empower the dog through the baby's presence.

The dog should be acknowledged during every visit made to the baby. Every time the dog sees the baby, they should be fed and most importantly, *acknowledged*. If the quality of your affection toward your dog suffers by the presence of the baby, then you could have a problem later. You don't want to shower your newborn with affection while ignoring your dog unless the dog is absent. The perception you want your dog to have is that they will benefit from the attention given to the baby. Once the dog feels that the baby preserves and even elevates their status, you will never have to worry again. Now you're making the baby indispensable because their presence results in additional praise and attention for your happy dog.

It's normal for a new mother to feel concerned about a big family dog leaning into a baby's crib. I get it. The key is to distract the dog to a source of reward before that happens. This way the dog is rewarded for approaching the baby but is intercepted before their proximity to the baby becomes uncomfortable for you. Over time, any hesitation you or your dog has will dissipate. The beauty of this process is you and your dog will eventually both feel comfortable with the new family dynamic. We don't ever want to exclude our dog from the joy we have for our baby. If our training focuses only on the positive behavior of your dog while minimizing emphasis on their mistakes, no bad feelings can simmer within your dog.

The household, including the baby and the dog, should operate like a football team. When there's a huddle, everybody is kept abreast of the plan. Nobody is outside of the circle. Keeping your dog in the circle gives them a sense of belonging that all children crave as well.

Most problems between family members come from a perception of inequity. If everyone feels they're being treated fairly, that's all that matters. Favoritism should be avoided at all costs.

Dogs can be great protectors of children and other dogs. The only way they become a protector is to feel vital toward that child or dog's welfare. I know. I grew up an only child in a household full of dogs. I always felt safety in their presence because they knew I needed their companionship. Don't we all want to feel needed? Feeling important to a dog isn't just about food or walking; it's about fairness.

CHAPTER TEN

WALKING YOUR DOG, A.K.A. NAVIGATING THE CONCRETE JUNGLE

To your dog, a walk is like Christmas morning. But as with everything else about dog training, there are certain do's and don'ts you want to be aware of.

Venturing outside the home with your dog can present many challenges, no matter how well-behaved your dog may be at home. It's one thing to know how *your* dog normally reacts to varying situations, but more challenging to accurately determine what the *other* dog and their owner may have in store for you.

The key to avoiding uncomfortable surprises on a walk is being aware of your surroundings when out with your dog. Probably due to my upbringing, I never go anywhere with my dog unless I have a plan. If I don't know where I'm going, it's much more difficult to assess the best way to get there. We may have to change our plan at some point but you can't change a plan you don't already have. Knowing what hurdles may be encountered long before they become reality is key. We simply want to recognize beforehand the signs of potential danger when venturing out with our best friend. We don't want to be like those pet owners who seem to be startled by everything. This leads them to overreact, thus leading their dog to do the same.

Every time I put the leash and training collar on my dog, there's a purpose. It could be because I'm about to train my dog. It could mean there's a car ride in store. It could also mean we're merely going for a walk. We never want our dog to know the reason hardware is being put on them. On the other hand, the more we know about our dog's behavioral tendencies, the better. Proper exposure to things, people, and other dogs will allow your pet to deal better with any unexpected situation.

Here in California, we have a statewide leash law. In some larger metro areas it can be strictly enforced. In other states without such laws, I still consider the leash and collar a necessity, based solely on safety concerns. Though it might seem amusing to have your dog ride on your lap in the car or stroll around unhindered at a public park, that careless overconfidence won't protect your dog from potential danger. Sometimes we must avoid spoiling our dogs when there are safety concerns. We must always consider the worst-case scenario.

When I served in the military, we always marched in formation. Our drill instructor had a plan for each day. Sometimes the plan was exactly like yesterday's plan; other times it took on a completely different approach. We didn't always know the plan, but the drill instructor always did. The day's plan was for the instructor to know and for the recruit to find out. When it comes to your dog, you're the drill instructor.

WALKING AROUND THE BLOCK

Assuming your dog has learned to accept other dogs, bicycles, passing cars, and strangers, the trick is determining what distractions should be avoided and which should be embraced. If you're walking your dog on leash, it's imperative that any other dog you meet also be on leash.

If your dog is on leash but the other dog is loose, the other dog has all the power. If your dog is off leash but the other dog is under control, then your dog has the power. Remember to keep your meetings like for like; where all dogs who first meet will either be all on-leash or all off-leash. This way everyone is on equal footing. It's the safest approach. Most of the dog fights I've randomly witnessed—and often been forced to separate—involved two or more unfamiliar dogs that were on unequal footing. It's normally a dog on leash that gets attacked by the unleashed dog. For this reason, I'm constantly on the lookout for signs of an unleashed dog before it's in flight toward us.

Before we discuss the signs of danger, let's review the process.

The first thing I do with my dog is put the leash on them well before we actually go walking. I don't want my dog charging out anxiously in anticipation of leaving the house. It doesn't matter what our destination is, we never want to telegraph our specific purpose when putting on the leash. If our dog is overly excited when leaving our house, it will often attract negative attention from neighbors and other passing dogs. Controlling our dog's momentum should be a constant concern.

When my dog has forgotten about the leash and settled down, then I will pick up the leash and head for the door. I want my dog to stop whenever possible, starting with the front door. Then it's the end of the porch. It isn't just for training, but also to prepare us for what may be around the corner. Having consistent control of our dog empowers us and gives us self-confidence. It also doesn't put us in a situation of having to regain control after it's already been lost.

Once we're walking calmly down the street, there are specific situations that bring me concern. Open garage doors and gates can be more alarming than a neighbor's front door being open. While all scenarios are reason for concern, a larger percentage of loose dogs come from an open garage than an open front door.

No matter how goal-oriented you and your dog are, it's unrealistic to expect that same preparation from other dog owners. The majority of dog walkers are simply clueless. Many are talking on their phone or handling more dogs at one time than is feasible. If you're struggling with your own dog—or dogs—how will you be prepared for a threat from another dog?

Even if you're unsure about that approaching dog on the sidewalk or the busy street next to you, it is *always* best to remain calm, even if your heart is racing. Form a strategy of how you will deal with each situation beforehand, as preparation will alleviate much of the uncertainty you and your dog encounter unexpectedly. If dating is like a job interview, then dog training is like a poker game. You never want to show excitement even if you're feeling it. Save that excited voice for a moment of praise or recall.

I often tell my clients to talk in a Ben Stein monotone about 80 percent of the time when working with their dog. When your dog reacts to anything, you can either confirm it by reacting yourself, or you can ignore it and act as if nothing happened. Just remember, to a dog, high voice means good. Low voice means bad. Loud voice serves no purpose at all. Silence tells your dog you don't care about what they're worried about. The less you care, the less they act out.

BE AWARE OF YOUR SURROUNDINGS

If you're looking at your dog instead of your incoming text message, you'll notice things about your dog you may have never recognized previously. Monitoring your dog's point of view makes you aware of things you might've overlooked with your subpar human hearing and non-canine telescopic vision. Your dog will tell you a lot in regard to what you *should* be worried about on the walk. Where are they looking? What is their body language telling you? Did they hear something you didn't?

Beware of situations where you're passing a large dog being kept in a yard surrounded by a fence that doesn't appear high enough to keep the dog from jumping over. In contrast, beware of scenarios where the fence isn't low enough to keep small dogs from crawling underneath it. By the same token, you don't want to be the person whose dog is running loose around the neighborhood. Maybe you didn't properly inspect the airtight integrity of your yard. These are signs we often pay very little attention to until something happens. There could be holes under the fence or in the fence itself. Not all oversights will lead to catastrophe, but it only takes one time.

Don't feel compelled to have your dog meet passing dogs just because someone says their dog is friendly. It's best to use your own intuition when it comes to canine introductions. Body language from your dog or from the other dog can be a very clear sign. A dog who is posturing should be avoided. Whether it's your dog or the other dog, make sure one isn't too eager to meet the other. All it takes is one dog to instigate an altercation.

Posturing can take many forms. Even if a dog isn't showing obvious signs like barking or growling doesn't mean they're ready to meet another dog. A dog with a wagging tail and a tongue hanging out when approaching another dog is the optimum sign. A dog with hackles standing on their spine, ears back, head down, mouth closed, or their tail between their legs, is one you might be better off avoiding. These are more subtle examples of aggression; other signs of aggression are much more obvious.

Since many of my training activities take place at public parks, there are a number of danger signs. We've already talked about generally avoiding unfamiliar dogs that are off-leash no matter where they appear. There are also times when even the appearance of a dog on-leash can spell potential mishaps. This tends to be the case when the dog seems to physically dominate their owner. I call this a canine mismatch. The two most common displays of canine mismatches involve elderly dog owners with large dogs, and small children entrusted with their family dog.

While most elderly owners are seen walking smaller dogs, there are exceptions. However, if you approach an elderly person with a dog that seems larger than they can comfortably control, this might be a duo you should avoid.

It's a common sight in my park training to encounter dogs on-leash, but being handled by small children. If I were playing the odds, I would give an 80 percent chance that the youngster will drop the leash at least once. Shortly thereafter you may find the loose dog running in your direction. If you only had a 20 percent chance of arriving safely on an airplane, would you take that flight?

I'm not saying all dogs that approach you off-leash or on-leash will lead to an altercation. I just make a habit of taking the path of least resistance. It's important that dogs meet other dogs whenever possible, just not when one dog has a clear advantage initially or is poorly behaved.

Taking your family dog to the groomer or vet is a fairly simple process for most people. Regardless of how many successful trips

I've taken in the past, there is always a possibility of running into the wrong dog at the wrong time. This is why I usually have someone else accompany me to open doors. This way I have both hands free if confronted by an agitated dog upon entering any particular establishment. This rule applies to trips to PetSmart or Petco as well. Just because dogs are there doesn't mean that they went willingly. A dog under stress is more likely to react negatively to people or other dogs entering a space unfamiliar to that nervous dog.

I'm not telling you this to create a fear of taking your dog out into the world, as exposure is among the greatest gifts you can give your best friend. I just want to make sure that you don't go out trusting everyone and their dog. Consider all newcomers to be guilty until proven innocent. Trust needs to be earned; like the faith awarded to your most trusted friends and family members.

If you could talk to as many clients as I have, you'd realize these canine altercations occur with great frequency, leaving both parties feeling responsible and embarrassed to talk about the incident. This means there are plenty of other incidents we don't hear about. Denial leads them to believe that the first time their dog goes rogue was simply an aberration. That same owner may be looking at the next dog meeting as a way to prove or disprove this theory. You don't want to be the guinea pig in somebody else's canine aggression experiment.

I use neighboring pets and passing people myself for training canine students that have leash aggression. I just always make sure that I have a training leash and collar on my dog when these temptations are realized. I also maintain a safe distance from any obvious distractions during training. Recall is the real test, especially with distractions being present. I believe that a dog must come reliably before ever being allowed off-leash. Everything else—"Stay" and "Heel"—come much more easily when a dog anticipates being called back without him or her ever knowing when. Most dogs are rather easy to call back when they're paying attention to you, but will they return when focused on something else?

When you begin working with your dog initially, it might seem like *your* dog's behavior is embarrassing; while other dogs seem comparatively well-behaved. But when your dog has mastered foundation training (Come, Stay, and Heel), the world will look a bit different. Suddenly you'll notice all the dogs that behave as yours once did. Behavior is relative and graded on a curve. The best way to assess your dog's progress is by comparing them with other dogs encountered. This is why behavior comes before training; training is just a tool to be used in enhancing good behavior.

While I'm a strong believer in using food for my training, I don't use it at all when meeting other dogs. Food can be a great equalizer when a dog is frightened by a trash truck, but less useful in the presence of new people and their dogs. One dog can never be rewarded in the presence of another dog unless that dog is also fed. It's the same kind of parity I use when meeting new dogs off- or on-leash. As a general rule, the less affection you give another dog—or yours—in the presence of other dogs the better. If the feedback given amidst a group of dogs remains neutral, you never have to think about correcting any resentment among the group. It's an all-or-nothing proposition.

Many of my clients have a desire to one day bring their dog to one of those fenced dog parks. They also want to take their dog to group "doggie daycare." While I've never taken any of my personal dogs to either place, there are some rules I should mention if taking your own dog into a canine group setting.

The concrete jungle is so vast that it includes grassy areas as well. While it's safe to assume that we will not be able to control the behavior of others—I don't even try—there are danger signs when taking your best friend to common canine meeting places. Having a short checklist of things to avoid on your first trip to such locations just may go a long way toward grief prevention.

The most important factor goes back to my "like for like" philosophy. When you immerse your dog into a group of new dogs, it's important that your dog isn't sporting a leash or training collar. It's safe to say that the other dogs will not be wearing one. Any dog that enters a group dog run wants to enter on even ground with the other dogs.

Small dogs should never be picked up in the presence of other dogs as that often attracts negative attention from the other dogs present. I've seen dogs pulled out of their owner's arms by other dogs simply because their owners don't understand the "bait" scenario. This basically says that no single dog should be the prime focus in a canine group setting. The goal is simply for our dog to fit in, which is to say they are out of sight and out of mind. Blending is always better than standing out.

This is why a neutral voice and body language will go far in avoiding resentment between any dogs in a group setting. No special attention should be given to any dog, including your own. The last thing dogs need is a biased referee deciding which dog is the most important. Think of it as a rock band where nobody has top billing.

Preparation is a key factor in any situation with your dog, especially if they lack life experience. Continued exposure will teach your dog how to deal with new situations. A calm dog will seldom get into altercations, even if they're surrounded by poorly behaved dogs. Good behavior is certainly contagious. Poorly behaved dogs tend to bring all the good dogs down a notch. Like anything else, being around pros helps you more than being in the company of rookies.

You want to gravitate toward dogs that are better behaved than your dog, or at least close to equal. This will elevate their behavior simply by association. I've seen very well-behaved dogs who don't really know what to do with canine troublemakers. They may withdraw completely from the new dog or they may issue a warning to the other dog. That behavior can be very mild or very intense. The last thing we want is our trusting dog to be attacked by a dog we encouraged them to meet. The bottom line is in simply choosing your dog's friends very carefully.

My clients often tell me that learning to anticipate possible events with their dog makes them more confident. Since we know a bad situation can degrade your dog's behavior, we should also assume that our confidence will decrease after being ambushed by a new situation. This is why I'm so passionate about structure with your dog.

Many times, dogs that bark and act out on walks feel that their owner isn't engaged enough to protect them, leading them to issue threats to dogs that you've overlooked. Whenever your dog does become focused on something we want to make sure that we acknowledge that threat. It's just like raising small children: Much of what they see or hear they want you to validate. If they think you didn't see it, they may become vocal in hopes of getting your attention.

Now that you know what to look for in your own concrete jungle, you won't find yourself blindsided. My hope is that if you are better prepared for taking your dog out, your confidence will soar. It certainly has worked for my clients. Structure helps all members of the family know their roles. Make sure that your best friend knows their role.

CHAPTER ELEVEN

TRAINING 2.0: ADDING SOME TRICKS TO OUR FOUNDATION TRAINING

With a basic understanding of canine obedience, expanding upon that should be a relatively easy task. A foundation built on "Come," "Stay," "Sit," and eventually "Lie down" will lead you on a natural path to teaching additional tricks from those basic positions. On the other hand, teaching tricks before basic obedience only leaves you with a dog built for the circus, but not for dependability as a pet.

Understanding that your dog must learn to stay before sitting, and sit before lying down, shows you're teaching everything in its natural sequence. You're building a strong foundation.

The last thing I want a trained dog to do is anticipate what the next trick will be. When commanding the dog to "Sit," it should not lead them to skip straight to "Lie down." It's logical that sitting should come before lying down since it's how they would perform these actions without your command. So, if I'm teaching "Sit," I won't introduce "Lie down" until they've perfected "Sit." This way when I say "Sit," they don't confuse it with any command that may follow.

I also like to give commands that contain different numbers of syllables for easier command recognition. Since "Lie down" comes directly after "Sit," it will have two syllables while the preceding command has only one. These don't seem like big things to you, but the dog normally isn't interpreting words as much as he is picking up sounds and verbal rhythm. We want to train with distinct commands and emotion consistent with what we're asking them to do. This is the same reason "Come" is used with a happy tone, while "Stay" requires a more stern tone. The words might mean something specific to us, but the tone and rhythm we use make interpretation easier for the dog. They operate more on emotion than logic.

Having been a movie trainer, I've spent a lot of time getting dogs to perform trained behaviors while looking natural doing it. Every canine movie story requires a dog to perform different natural behaviors on cue. When doing the Lassie series, my grandfather Rudd was always opposed to Lassie performing scripted behaviors that any other dog wouldn't do naturally. Lassie wouldn't fly, answer telephones, talk, or do anything the average dog would not be inclined to do. He never wanted Lassie to appear cartoonish, but rather be the perfect average dog. Part of Lassie's appeal was that any of us could envision our dog enduring a similar adventure. Rudd avoided the possibility of making Lassie appear mechanical, meaning every behavior had a motivation behind it. This is why my family and I have never taught "Sit" before the command to "Stay" has been perfected from a standing position.

Keeping this in mind, there should always be a reason for your dog to sit; not simply to make them stay better. If you need a dog to sit in order to stay, then chances are the stay is less than dependable. A standing stay is more impressive because it's easier for the dog to break. I have to shake my head whenever I see dog owners making their dog sit every time they stop when stopping itself, not sitting, is the goal. Each position should be seen as a path to the next trick. Why make a dog sit at an intersection when they will have to get up and walk as soon as the light turns green anyway?

The best way to look at furthering your dog's education is to look at each position as a starting point, beginning with a standing stay. The standing stay isn't only impressive but is also the best position from which to call your dog for the quickest response. Too often when you call a dog out of any stay position it can damage the quality of their stay. A simple way to restore the stay is to always put the dog back on their starting point after recall and make them stay a bit longer. This way the dog doesn't begin to anticipate coming the next time you command them to stay. Dogs are experts at recognizing a pattern. If you always do something in a particular order, they will continue to do things in that order until you change it.

Everything that emerges from my training begins with the mark. You might remember that the mark can be any defined area that's approved for your dog to stay. This is how I teach dogs the concept of "Stay" without confusing it with any commands that follow. If you talk to anyone who's had their dog trained, most will not have a dog that stays unless it includes sitting. There's plenty of time to teach that command *after* the dog has mastered the concept of stay. Look at each position as a base like on a baseball diamond.

FIRST BASE

This is the standing position previously mentioned. Dogs tend to focus on their front feet so those are the only two that *must* be on the mark. Since the goal is to get your dog to recognize even the smallest mark, keeping all four feet on that mark can be somewhat impractical. A mark may be as large as a football field or as small as a dime.

Now envision all the things your dog can learn from the standing position. They can learn to put their feet up on a wall or a rock. They can learn to stop from a walking position. They can be taught to "Pick it up" and "Bring it here." They can be taught to "Dig" or "Limp." They can be taught to turn to the right or left, bow, or back up. These are all behaviors that logically begin from a standing position. If your dog is already sitting then you would have to teach them "On your feet" just to get them out of their "auto sit." I will eventually teach "On your feet" to all dogs anyway, but only to bring them out of a sit or lie down command I actually gave.

We want to keep our training flowing in a logical sequence that doesn't confuse your canine companion. It will also keep you on track in your training. Then you will be led along in your training by concentrating on each base separately. I'm very methodical in my training and I find it keeps both the dog and my training on a clear path.

You'll know when your first base lesson has gone too long when your dog begins wanting to sit or lie down from boredom or fatigue. This would be a good time to give your dog a brief break (recess); once you've restored them to their original standing position. This "On your feet" command is achieved by taking one foot and placing it gently under your dog's hindquarters while holding the leash in place (see illustration on page 141).

You must send the message that recess will not begin when they're tired but rather when you say so. This way the lesson is ended only upon them resuming the original position. After your dog has cleared his or her mind on their recess, you might want to move to second base for their next lesson. While starting the dog on a standing stay, we will then give the command to sit. The "Sit" command is simply holding the leash in place while gently pushing their butt down (see illustration of "Sit"). Make sure your dog isn't permitted to sit or lie down until *you* actually give the command. We want to leave the dog with the memory that it was our idea, even if they wanted to do it anyway. They can never be left feeling that we will not enforce any command we give them, no matter how insignificant it may seem at the time.

As I've mentioned, we always want to keep the lessons to fifteen to twenty minutes at a time initially. Possibly less for a standing stay, since a dog will tire of this position more rapidly. We always give ourselves the option of offering a food reward periodically for stay and upon the dog assuming any new position on your command. Some dogs are very sensitive to physical praise while on a "Stay," so I find food to be the best reward for that. Sometimes petting them on a stay is equivalent to releasing them, in their mind. It's best to feed the dog with one hand while using the verbal and hand signal for stay simultaneously (see illustration of "stay" hand signal).

SECOND BASE

Now that you've done a lesson on first base, it would be a good time to mix it up and begin with a new base. Starting with your dog on a standing stay, we would now give them the command to "Sit." This is normally a more comfortable position for all but the most high-strung dogs (the "go" dogs). This would be the launching position for tricks like "Shake/High five" and "Sit up." These are the primary basic tricks that stem from the "Sit" position. Second base offers fewer avenues to other tricks but is important for other reasons.

When I was in the military we had two basic positions when we were in parade formation: Attention and At Ease. I consider a dog performing a standing stay to be the equivalent of standing at attention while sit would more closely resemble at ease. Sit is something that should be earned by standing at attention well. Sitting is a more comfortable position, so staying there should not require as much effort to maintain.

Even when you're trying to get to the next training base, never skip the previous one. If you want your dog ultimately to "Sit," we still don't want the dog to assume that position until we actually request it. This way the sequence of commands remains consistent with our starting position and we are never skipping positions. Dogs pattern easily so skipping positions will lead them to anticipate the last position they learned. If dogs could read books, they would only be interested in the last chapter. We must make it worthwhile to read the rest of the book. Reward the dog at every base initially. If they skip a base, take them back to the previous base and reward them there. Never reward a dog for going where they already want to go. Reward the effort, not the skill.

THIRD BASE

"Lie down" is by far the most satisfying of all the bases for the mellow ("stay") dogs, but not always for the "go" dogs. The very active dogs will present more of a challenge here. There are many ways to extend the training from this position. Third base represents the best starting point for commands like "On your side," "Head down," "Roll over," and "Crawl."

In fact, I often add a trick like "Head down" or "Crawl" even when my clients haven't requested it. Why? I've found that if a dog is having problems staying on a "Lie down," teaching the next trick can make them stay better. Teaching a dog to do something that can only be achieved from one base position shifts the focus from getting up (leaving their base) to performing the next trick. In essence, the dog is again thinking about the last chapter of the book instead of putting the book down.

SMALL BITES

All training is best achieved in small bites. Keep the goals achievable. Whenever I see a plate overflowing with food, I think *there's no way I can eat all that*. However, when I see a small plate, I clean it and often ask for seconds. Training should be done in stages that allow you and your dog to be rewarded periodically and frequently. Try not to overwhelm your dog with too much at once. Keep your training goals achievable.

Your dog voluntarily staying in *any* of these positions when under duress is a sign of progress. A dog standing on a curb barking at another dog will eventually become a dog just standing on a curb. Then from there it will evolve into a dog sitting on the curb. Then when they're no longer agitated, they will typically lie down because eventually they become bored with not being able to act upon their fear and/or anxiety. We could call this *acceptance*.

If I tell an agitated dog to sit and ignore another dog, it's a bit like being chained while underwater. The dog is naturally more agitated because being on a "Stay" makes them feel much more vulnerable than if they had more freedom to react to what they perceive as possible danger. Freedom gives the dog options and makes them feel more comfortable that they can maneuver around whatever may transpire.

I'm sure it's a product of my upbringing, but I find it very easy to put myself in the dog's situation. How would I feel if I were only given one choice for every situation? How would you react when your back is up against the wall? These are the things any intuitive dog owner must consider. It's the narcissistic owner who thinks, *It's not bothering me, so it must be okay.* When you get inside a dog's head, you begin to see things through their eyes. Take it from someone who ate Liv-a Snaps as a kid and crawled around on the floor like a dog, even after learning how to walk.

The purpose in giving you this information isn't to encourage you to teach circus tricks to your dog. The purpose is to put you in a position to go beyond the training necessities should you choose to do so. Breaking down the training into sections not only simplifies things for your dog, but for the owner/trainer as well. My grandfather Rudd wrote a training book many years ago and the brilliance of Rudd's book is that he broke down his tricks into three sections: Elementary School, High School, and College.

The definition of a trained dog is different for everybody. Rudd and my father taught Lassie hundreds of commands for the needs of the TV series and movies. However, other show dogs were prepared for projects based on the behaviors they would need to know for that particular project. Each time a dog learns a new behavior, it's a foundation for what you teach later, no matter what it is. The intelligence of a dog seems to increase with every command they're taught. The cruelest thing a dog owner can do is to neglect the natural talents of your canine companion. Dogs want structure and crave learning. It's our enthusiasm toward training that determines how much they will embrace training. There is no such thing as a dumb dog—only an unmotivated one.

Another purpose in using these bases is to reveal the strengths and weaknesses of your dog. Some will be more proficient on one base than another. One base may lead to a couple of new commands while another may yield half a dozen new behaviors, depending on the dog. Even if you never go beyond the basics with your dog, knowing the bases will make those foundational behaviors stronger.

In an extension of this chapter I want to introduce many of my favorite "parlor tricks." These tricks are the ones I often teach my clients as a bonus. Every one of these tricks can be taught from any of the bases described in this chapter.

MY FAVORITE MOVIE TRICKS THAT ARE FUN TO TEACH

Working in the movie industry for nearly a decade and a half, I was called upon to teach tricks to various dogs that a typical dog owner might never desire their dog to do in normal home life. I've trained natural behaviors like "Dig," "Speak," "Lift your leg," and "Tear it up" on cue—behaviors your dog regrettably may do too often on their own already. Instead of teaching these somewhat annoying behaviors, these "parlor tricks" are gags that may not be as essential as some other movie tricks but are great for showing off when hosting a dinner party.

Before I introduce my favorite tricks, I should explain a little bit about which tricks are the most useful for dogs working in movies and TV. While dogs may be called upon to do any number of behaviors, the most vital tricks typically are "Come," "Speak," "Go with," "Retrieve," and "Stay"—in all positions. These are tricks that form the basis of my obedience training platform, with the only additions being "Go with," "Speak," and "Retrieve." These three commands I've used primarily while working in the film industry. There isn't as much use for them at home unless a dog is needed to bring things to the owner, giving "Retrieve" added importance.

Why are those tricks so important for film work? Since most dog movies portray the canine star interacting with humans, "Go with" is simply teaching the dog to go with a person other than the trainer. It's like a "Heel" on someone else. The other two main movie tricks, "Speak" and "Retrieve" are basically the ways a dog communicates with their human costars on film.

If you have a dog that can do these three things plus the basics from a good distance, you have a dog that has the foundation to work in film. While Lassie was eventually trained to perform well over one hundred different behaviors for the demands of that long-running show, these were the three trained behaviors you saw Lassie doing in almost every episode. She would "Speak" to tell us something. Then if we didn't understand, she would bring us something ("Retrieve"). She would spend the rest of her time traveling with various people. The "Go with" command made us believe that Lassie belonged with those people. These are tricks that could easily be the basis of another book, so for the time being I'll teach some flashier tricks that can be taught rather quickly.

The first two tricks are ones that can be taught from a standing stay position (see illustration of "standing stay").

The first trick is one that's great for repositioning your dog when they come forward from their mark. It comes in handy on a movie set when the goal is to move the dog while limiting physical contact with them. Before teaching *any* new commands, make sure the dog is wearing their training leash and collar. Remember that familiar Weatherwax phrase, "the leash comes off when the dog is trained." I have practiced that philosophy for as long as I can remember.

Back Up

This trick can be taught quickly with most dogs. It's simply the act of a dog moving backward in a straight line, on cue. The physical (hand) cue for the command is to brush your hands toward the dog while also giving the verbal command "Back up."

While you're giving your dog this command, you'll begin to walk straight into your dog. You should hold the leash loose enough so that it doesn't hinder the backward progress of your dog. They normally will begin moving back simply to avoid being stepped on (which you are implying with your feet). If your dog has an "auto-sit," this command will be somewhat complicated. The moment your dog sits, no more backing up can occur. If this is the case, then you must teach your dog "On your feet," which is simply taking one foot and threatening to step on the rear toe of your dog. You will pick up the leash at this point so they're unable to back away from your foot correction.

Remember that physical correction is only implied. Worst case scenario, you may have to touch their foot with yours. There is never a reason to actually step on the dog's foot. When your foot goes under their body they will most likely rise, at which time you'll reward them

for coming out of a sit. Once the dog is standing again, you can continue cueing the dog to "Back up." "On your feet" is also the command seen in movies when a dog implies urgency by rising from a sitting position. This is canine "acting." The physical command is bringing one hand back like you're pulling back with a leash while bringing one foot forward.

Sometimes the dog will back up willingly, but not in a straight line. If this occurs, you should find a wall and another piece of furniture to funnel the dog backward. A wall can be used in conjunction with something like a chair to provide a solution for a crooked "back up." Walk the dog into a position where those obstructions are on each side. Repeat the command and begin walking into the dog. The combination of wall and chair will force the dog to back up straight. Reward the dog at the end of their journey backward. This should be repeated until the obstructions are no longer needed for the dog to back up properly. This can be tested periodically. The obstructions can be added again if the dog regresses for any reason—having a setback in training is never an issue. You simply pick up at the point a mistake was made by either you or the dog and resume from there. Don't be afraid to take one step back to take two steps forward. It's bound to happen at some juncture of your training, there's no need to be frustrated by it.

Turn to the Right and Left

This is actually considered two separate tricks, but the process of training each is nearly identical. Since I'm predominantly right-handed, I tend to begin teaching "turn to the right" first. I want to concentrate only on the right turn until it's mastered. I will not introduce the "turn to the left" until I'm done teaching the other direction. This way there's no confusion from the dog in performing the commands separately later.

The easiest way to begin this trick is to take a tantalizing goody and show it to your dog. Then you simply want to lead the dog's nose with that hand toward their tail and then bring that treat along the opposite side of their body. They are basically doing a "360" going to their right. Only when the dog completes the revolution will you "pay" them.

Now that they're facing you again, we will repeat the right circle, rewarding only upon completion. Eventually you won't need the goody anymore but will simply make the same hand command that you used when you *were* holding a dog treat. Then from there we will combine the verbal command "Turn to the Right" with the hand command and extend our distance from the dog gradually each time we give the command.

You might notice that I didn't suggest using the leash to teach this trick initially since it could hinder the movement of a dog who's already turning willingly. However, sometimes you'll run into a dog that just won't follow the goody all the way around, or simply stands there looking at you. If this happens, there's an easy solution, but the training leash and collar will now have to be placed on the dog. Once the leash is attached, take the handle and bring it around their rear end and to the other side. You're now in a position to turn your dog manually like a top. When pulling the dog gently around, keep your leash hand parallel to the dog's spine and simply reward when they've completed the circle. Eventually you won't need the leash to get them to do this. They should become proficient with you leading them through the circle before trying it with the leash off. Then you can incorporate the hand command with the verbal command already being used.

Now that your dog has learned turning to their right, it should be that much easier to get them to turn the opposite way. Everything you did to get the dog to turn to their right will just be reversed now. All the same techniques will be used. Personally, I like to use my right hand to cue the right turn and my left to cue turning in that direction. This makes it clear to the dog when you begin cuing him or her using only the hand command. I teach both the verbal and physical commands simultaneously with all tricks so that I can use one or the other depending on which is more convenient at any given moment. The verbal and hand command should become interchangeable.

Crawl

This command and "Speak" I consider the easiest behaviors to teach a dog, though other trainers may disagree. I've taught dogs to crawl on more than a few movie gigs. My dog, Betty, crawled under fire with a notebook in her mouth for the movie "Top Dog." It's not an essential for movies, but the trick has enjoyed some cinematic moments. Unlike "Back up" and turning to the right and left, "Crawl" is taught from a lie-down position. The best place for you to begin training this is on the floor with your dog. Being on the floor yourself will make it less tempting for your dog to rise from the "Lie down" position. The leash will be worn when teaching this trick. Once the dog is lying down, you want to make sure the leash is worn to the side so the dog doesn't get it caught on their legs when moving forward.

Now that you're on the floor and your dog is in the lying position, you will give the dog the command to "Crawl." The hand signal we will incorporate with the verbal command is extending the fingers toward the dog. Food can be concealed and offered when they advance toward you without rising to their feet.

The moment the dog begins moving toward your extended "cuing" hand, the food reward will come right behind it and be given to the

dog directly. You don't want your reward hand to come from above the dog's head as this will lead the dog to rise out of the lying position. As your dog extends his neck and body to get the treat, his hind legs should become extended behind him or her (like a frog). This is the sign that your dog is getting the trick. This behavior is nearly impossible to achieve if the dog is uncomfortable dragging their belly across the floor. Make sure the surface you're teaching your dog on is one that has traction and is soft, like grass or carpeting. Tile and slippery wood floors aren't a good place to introduce this trick. Remember, in the beginning you want the crawl to be as easy to achieve as possible, then increase the difficulty level and distance over time.

Once the dog is performing the crawl comfortably, you can begin to stand up while still keeping your cuing hand low and close to the dog's nose. Little by little you can raise your "cuing" hand until you're extending your fingers toward the dog at about knee level while merely leaning toward your dog.

Some dogs will want to rise to get the goody rather than advance from the crawling position to get paid. If this is the problem, you might need to implement a piece of furniture into your training much like when you were teaching "Back up." This time rather than using the furniture to funnel the dog back, you will use a prop to keep the dog from rising to their feet. You don't want to impede their forward progress; you just want them to advance without standing. The best tools for this seem to be a coffee table or chair, depending on the size of the dog. You're basically creating a bridge over the dog that actually gives the dog no other option than to crawl under it. This may require some creativity on your part in finding a bridge that doesn't allow a dog to stand or walk under it.

While these four tricks will create the basis of a great little dog-and-pony show, it wouldn't be fair to not reveal at least one of those essential movie tricks mentioned previously. The trick I relied on

most often for film was one of those natural behaviors that you cannot force a dog to do.

Dogs bark all the time, yet seldom when you actually ask for it. Like "Yawn" or "Sneeze" a dog cannot be made to "Speak." These behaviors can only be induced. Most of my clients' dogs have been taught to speak but not because the owners wanted them to speak; rather the exact opposite. I simply put a cue on those moments when they barked anyway. Sometimes they barked at a knock on the door. Sometimes they barked at something happening outside a window. Sometimes the dogs were just very nervous and any quick movement on my part could induce a bark from them.

In response, I would simply put a hand signal on the behavior and say "Speak" while the dog was already barking. The hand signal I use is a closed hand with just my index finger unclenched and raised straight up. I would then offer a goody to the dog since now I'm cuing the barking. This will normally cause the dog to pause from their barking to eat the goody. After eating it, they'll often go right back to barking again. I will once again cue the behavior and reward them for the barking that occurs *after* I've given the verbal and/or hand signal. When your dog is speaking to your verbal or physical command—and not the mailman or some other distraction—you have

taught your dog to speak. While your dog is learning to speak, you will be redirecting their bark from something else. The barking directed toward other distractions will eventually disappear. Dogs tend to lose interest in doing something that they can no longer claim as their idea. It's just the way dogs think.

My dad always said, "The best way to get a dog to shut up is to get them to speak on cue." What did he mean? While he seldom explained to me the reasons he did things, I spent a lot of time figuring them out myself. I learned that a dog who speaks on cue will be barking for the right reason—because we asked for it. We will be redirecting the barking. Now he or she won't be barking because they're afraid or aggressive. Elimination of the barking doesn't have to be our goal.

We're simply changing the reason and the motivation for barking; since most barking comes from a place of fear, your ability to convert this into an opportunity for the dog to be rewarded changes the tone and intensity of their bark. Now it begins to come from a happy place since it's now associated with food and love. It also serves as a distraction from the original catalyst of their barking. The dog is thinking, *oh food . . . what was I barking about?*

Dogs have short attention spans, so the food will temporarily disorient them. Once they rediscover the reason for their previous barking, they will recommence and you will recue the "Speak." Then you will reward. Wash, rinse, and repeat.

When you give the verbal command for "Speak" it will come with an excited, happy voice. I call it the you-can-do-it voice. It's a bit like a loud whisper. It's the voice of encouragement. Using an enticing and happy voice rhythm, without being firm, the more likely it will overpower another distraction.

I've found myself jumping up and down on movie sets getting a dog to speak when I was unable to use a verbal command and major distractions existed. I would use any tool—stomping my foot, snapping my fingers—that would keep the dog's attention on me. Barking requires focus and enthusiasm on the dog's part. If your dog speaks in a quiet place but not near distractions, then you've discovered why training dogs for film can be difficult.

Fear isn't always the motivation for a dog to bark. Another strong catalyst for barking is frustration. It could be frustration over being temporarily separated from someone. It could come from wanting a toy or any cherished item and not being able to get it. If you can harness either the fear or the frustration, you can teach your dog to speak.

Frustration is the tool you will use to teach the "brave" or "quiet" dogs. These are the dogs that you forget even have a voice. They don't bark at much of anything. The brave dogs don't bark naturally, because they're comfortable in their own skin. The quiet dogs don't bark because he or she doesn't want to draw any adverse attention their way. These are the dogs that are the hardest to teach to "Speak."

The good news with these dog personality types is they often have at least one thing they get truly excited about. Food seems like an obvious temptation to bark, but it depends on the appetite of that particular dog. The dog that isn't food crazy might go crazy over a particular toy. The dog that cares about neither may be enticed to bark by being left in a room by themselves or on the lonely side of a screen door.

If food is the tool of choice, then the dog needs to be mildly teased with it. Waving the goody by their face and not letting them have it can create a little excitement. The dog might even try jumping up on you to get the treat sooner. Whenever they try, we deflect them using a leg or arm. This will create even more frustration as more attempts to steal the food fail. The enticing you-can-do-it voice will be employed in conjunction with the unobtainable goody. Using a little hissing sound in your voice can often get a dog to bark when they're on the verge but not quite speaking. The verbal cue will always be soft in volume; the use of a firm voice will often intimidate the dog from barking at all. Sometimes getting up on a bench or someplace the dog can't reach you can add even more frustration. Trainer Karl Miller even went so far as to bark himself to induce a bark from the dog.

The second the dog makes even a peep, you will lavish them with food and praise. Any attempt they make to bark should be rewarded. If the bark never rises above a whisper, you won't pay them until they bring their volume up. Make sure the dog is acoustically okay with the room you're using to teach "Speak." Sometimes a dog will get an echo from their own voice that will discourage further barking—like in a bathroom or garage. The kitchen provides a great location for teaching speak since food being prepared on a counter can often induce a bark even before you ask for it. Remember that any attempt by the dog to steal the reward should be thwarted with your body, not your hand.

The favorite toy would be used the same way. That toy should be generously displayed and talked about, but not given. In essence, you're stoking a fire you might normally want extinguished. Try not to feel bad about teasing your dog with food or a toy as the reward you give them after they "Speak" will wash all the frustration away, at which time you will rebuild it again.

Eventually you won't need to create a volcano in your dog to get them to speak. Once they become strong speaking for the verbal command, you'll be able to cue the command with just the index finger. It's all about building consistency and distance with either a verbal or physical cue with every trick you teach your dog. Training is all about starting close and moving farther and farther away while still being able to get them to work like you were still standing right in front of them.

My experience observing obedience training is that it often never progresses beyond a few feet from the dog. I want you to always keep the big picture in mind. Envision what kind of distance you would like to ultimately see, and go for that. Never be content achieving the absolute minimum in the way of distance.

CHAPTER TWELVE

THE TAIL END OF THE LONG LEASH

When Lassie went off the air in 1974, my father had been assisting Rudd for eleven of the twenty seasons Lassie was on the air. Later, when working for Lou Schumacher, dad became disenchanted with constantly being assigned poorly trained dogs and somehow getting them to perform magic on a movie set with little preparation. Dad recognized that he would rather have his own handful of well-trained dogs than access to acres of dogs with limited training. He believed that only the trained dog should get the job; not necessarily the best-looking ones.

He ended up starting Weatherwax Trained Dogs. Early on he engaged in a short-lived partnership with Dennis Grisco, another accomplished movie trainer. Dennis also had a son, William, who has been my friend since our fathers became partners in 1977. The two of us learned how to train dogs the way most movie trainers learned back then. There weren't any movie dog training schools back in those days—it was somewhat of a lost art passed down by previous generations. Before writing this book, I asked William what advice he would give someone training their dog for the first time. He didn't hesitate in his answer: "Get the dog away from you as soon as possible."

While I knew exactly what he meant, the concept seems foreign to many obedience trainers who've never been forced to work very far from their dogs. Many non-movie trainers want their canine students to be right by their side or just a foot or two in front of them. Many of those same trainers don't even own a fifteen-foot or longer training lead. What are they trying to do exactly?

While control is certainly one training goal, there is also a freedom allotment that must be passed to your dog. Your dog must not only learn to obey, but also learn to make good decisions. This won't happen if you're afraid to allow your dog to make a mistake. Preventing your best friend from making errors won't develop responsible independent thinking. It's through making bad decisions that your dog learns to make better ones in the future. Obedience from a distance is always more useful than hovering over your dog during their schooling.

Considering the goal of most dog owners is to have a dog that's dependable on and off leash, getting your dog to "go deep" is the first step in achieving that goal. Going deep is putting your dog in a challenging position and welcoming their mistakes. This is how you can perfect "stay" and "recall," the two foundation commands most dependent on distance. Your dog will achieve perfection by being corrected for not coming or reset if breaking the stay position.

Maybe this entails having your dog stay from across the street. It could be having your dog come from far away without repeating your command. It could simply mean having a dog that will heel without needing a leash to accomplish it.

Why is a long leash better than a short one? It allows you to get that distance on your foundation training without worrying about losing control, at least during the early stages of your training. That feeling of not having control often leads your dog to exploit a lack of confidence. It's all about your confidence as a trainer. The long leash will give you the peace of mind needed.

If your dog is on a long stay, the end of the leash is never very far from your foot. Even if they decide to run, you'll be in a position to step on the leash before it's too late. Then we simply bring them back to their place of origin. You won't be able to do that with a short leash. By the time you recover your student, they'll have forgotten where they were supposed to be. You will appear more in control to your dog if you aren't visibly worried about what they're going to do. It's a three-step process. First you're holding the leash; then you aren't holding the leash. Eventually you will have the ability to remove the leash and still maintain control. Since your dog is already used to being away from you, they're less likely to bolt the second they leave your side. There will be no release of tension like a dog would feel if they were being disconnected from a short leash.

Let's review each element of what I call "Foundation Training" and see how to elevate it to becoming an off-leash command. The key is minimizing the meaning of the leash when it comes off. The first time it comes off will be in a controlled situation, like a fenced yard. We don't want to introduce off-leash training in an uncontrolled area where there's too much stimulus, though that's the eventual goal. First, we want our dog to master "Stay," "Come," and "Heel" where we're in a position to quickly put the leash back on if they fail.

Let's begin with "Stay." Since we're using a long leash in all of our outside training, we'll begin the stay with the leash on and in a controlled situation. When we feel ready to begin taking the leash off we will do so, and leave that leash beside them. Subliminally the dog will think they aren't completely free with the leash still nearby. We don't want to draw much attention to the act of taking the leash off; it should be a "throw away." This means that there should be no verbal feedback given to the dog to telegraph the fact they're now free to run away. We also don't want to emphasize the leash removal to our dog by rolling it up and putting it somewhere.

I'll then test the stay using as many distractions as possible. You want to simulate the distractions they're most likely to encounter on your outside excursions. If your dog reacts to people, there should be people present during training. If they react to other dogs, then there should be dogs present during their training. Whatever you believe will distract your dog on the street is exactly what you want to simulate in the yard. I will test my dog's stay from both a mark and from a specific position such as sitting or lying down.

Once you've achieved close to a 100 percent success rate in the backyard, you can begin to introduce them to a stay in a place without the security of fences. I want to continue desensitizing my dog to the act of taking off the leash, a process we began in the controlled scenario. Since the long leash is on initially, I'll take it off only after a series of "feints." Feinting is a term I use that simulates the removing of the leash by going to take it off. I will reach for the snap connecting the leash to their collar and snap it as if removing it, but then leaving it on. That sound will typically trigger our canine student to break. Over time our best friend will begin believing the snapping sound is merely a bluff. That's exactly what we want. We want them to lose trust in their own assumptions. We want them to be at a loss when it comes to predicting what we'll do. Then we simply trigger bad behavior through distractions so it doesn't become a problem when our dog is placed in a future uncontrolled situation. The more corrections you make in the yard, the stronger the stay will be outside the yard.

If our student is a hard case, I might resort to using two long leashes connected to their collar initially. This way I can take one long leash and throw it to the ground while still having control with the leash still being worn. The key here is to trigger the sound of freedom while maintaining a backup leash. When the bluff no longer triggers our best friend to attempt breaking their stay, we can begin taking both leashes off simultaneously and laying them on the ground. The dog will lose trust in the prospect of outsmarting you and will eventually forfeit any resistance. If you encounter distractions when your dog is off leash, the throw-chain distraction (jingling it) can provide an additional line of defense should they become distracted. Remember no plan is perfect without a backup plan.

Then there is recall. Much like our off-leash stay, it will begin in a controlled situation. The only difference here is that I'll leave the long leash dragging initially and incorporate the throw-chain distraction—if our dog fails to return reliably. Remember the throw-chain will be less effective if you've neglected using it previously.

If needed, the chain should be shaken in conjunction with your verbal command. Should they fail to come to the sound of the chain and/or command, then it should be thrown behind them, while repeating "Come." If your dog returns promptly then the long leash can be removed and the throw chain can be put away. Never forget to reward lavishly—both with food and voice. The long leash and throw chain will only be revealed again if your dog fails to come "freestyle" in the future.

Remember the throwing of the chain should always come by surprise, with the verbal command coinciding with its *landing*, not its release from your hand. Even if they've seen you with the chain in your hand previously it will surprise them, assuming they've never seen it actually *leave* your hand. The element of surprise is the key to the power of the throw chain. Remember to always "pay" your dog enthusiastically upon their return as this will erase any negative feeling from the throwing of the chain—or comparable distraction. Most importantly, repetition with pay will expedite the commands' reliability moving forward.

Remember that when your dog is called while you're standing still, they tend to come with less urgency. Always try to draw them toward you by creating some momentum in the direction you'd like them to go. Use an enthusiastic tone for come and a neutral tone for the stay. Obviously kneeling helps with come, while pursuit of your dog often leads to them trying to evade you.

It's very important to use as light a training lead as possible. You want it to be light because this will make its eventual removal less noticeable. Use the same bluffing techniques you've used for stay. You want to fake clicking off the long lead prior to actually removing it. It's also a good idea to feed your dog while actually detaching the lead from the collar, even when you're bluffing. This will turn the focus from the outside world back to you. Use food liberally until recall becomes automatic. Even afterwards, sporadic reward remains desirable for maintenance of the previous training. Remember training never ends and if you don't exercise the training its quality will erode over extended periods of neglect. Many dogs can be untrained as quickly as they are trained. If in the future they choose not to come in any specific situation, recreate that situation after putting the leash back on. This way you can quickly enforce the command under duress. Even if your dog comes ten straight times off-leash, one fail will earn the return of the long leash. Never be afraid to nip disobedience before it becomes a habit.

Teaching your dog to heel should always come after a strong recall has been attained. I've always believed that recall and heel go hand in hand. In fact, I remind my clients that heel is useless to teach in the absence of a quality recall. The reason the two commands are connected is because calling a dog to your side is the starting point for a dog walking by your side.

Whatever side you choose to have your dog heel should be the side to which they are called. It should also be the only side where they will be "paid." If your dog ever gets too far ahead or behind you while walking, recall will bring them back to your side at which time they will be paid.

The first step in achieving a strong off-leash heel is to begin putting the far end of your long line in your pocket. This way you'll be able to step on the remaining leash if they begin pulling. The key is that they won't see you doing anything with your hands while the leash is still connected to your body.

Once your best friend has mastered walking by your side hands-free, we can begin thinking of doing the same thing leash-free. Just as we did with stay, we want to have the leash remain present when they first have the freedom to run. The technique I use is to attach the long leash to my belt and drag it behind me. Doing this leaves the dog wondering whether the leash is actually still attached to them. The previous constant clicking on and off with the leash will keep them off-balance while keeping you in control. If at any point they fail to progress with the steps, we must go back to the previous step. For example, if they drift when completely off leash, you must go back to being connected with the leash in your pocket. If they fail with the leash in your pocket, you must go back to having the leash in your hand. Don't be afraid to take a step back in your training as it will only make the overall training stronger in the long run. The mistakes your dog makes are like money in the bank when it comes to future off-leash dependability.

Remember that your body is a powerful weapon. If your dog is heeling close to you, it is your body that will keep them from crossing over to the wrong side. It's also your body that can be used as a buffer against any seemingly aggressive behavior on a walk. Using your hand to control aggression can result in getting bitten inadvertently.

Training and caring for your dog can require a lot of practice. Patience is the key. You should train your dog the way you drive your car. Accidents can be avoided by simply allowing enough time to get to your destination. My popularity as a dog trainer isn't based on being expedient—it lies in being thorough. I never take shortcuts unless they're presented to me by the dog. Some dogs learn quicker. Each dog has a different aptitude and skill set. There is no other dog like the one you have by your side or on your lap.

Working dogs in movies could be a thankless job at times. Directors never seem to care much about how the dog feels, only that they perform the scripted action. This could lead movie trainers to take shortcuts that could sometimes put a dog's safety in jeopardy. I know. I've been there. I know what it's like to bring a well-trained dog to the set only for the scriptwriters to spring something on us at the last minute.

While I enjoyed the rush of getting movie dogs to perform under pressure, I find training dogs privately more rewarding. Private owners appreciate the power of humane training. They don't look at their dogs as tools, but companions. They appreciate the fact I don't rely on shock or force to achieve good behavior. I may threaten force but I never apply it. There's certainly nothing wrong with a dog believing you will use force, even if you never do. Dogs respond to threats much better than many people. They typically don't want to find out if the threat is real or not. This is where your acting ability can be an asset.

CHAPTER THIRTEEN

KEEPING YOUR DOG HEALTHY AND HAPPY

There are plenty of seemingly innocent things we do that can endanger our dogs that all dog owners ought to be aware of. Growing up in a family where dog welfare was literally priority number one, I learned basic rules early on that could prevent canine disaster. Even though we lived in a small house in the San Fernando Valley, for much of my childhood Dad broke the rules on the maximum number of dogs allowed in a single residential dwelling. We not only cared for three dogs and one or two cats of our own, but for months at a time we also rotated other dogs that my dad would be preparing for some TV or film project.

These transient dogs living with us were males that had to be kept away from our resident male dogs—dogs purposelessly kept unneutered. One door left open at the wrong time could result in a dog fight between two male dogs who had never met. It was like musical chairs 24/7, until my father started his own business in 1977.

Dad was unparalleled as a movie trainer, but was obsessed with the belief that neutering a dog would damage their disposition permanently. The rub was that most of the outside dogs in the film industry were also male dogs, just like Lassie. Lassie was just the first of the many female dog impersonators in movies and TV.

My private training practice constantly puts me in the position of not only mentoring dogs but also offering advice to their owners. It isn't just my work with a training leash that keeps me in high demand. I also consider myself to be a "Canine Counselor," as I frequently offer advice on many things that have absolutely nothing to do with training a dog. Flying in the face of my dad's reluctance to neuter dogs, I have always been an advocate of neutering male dogs, but no earlier than ten months. I feel there's a certain amount of beneficial hormonal development that occurs with young male dogs, but I agree with most veterinarians' opinions regarding the ultimate health benefits of neutering and spaying. These benefits can include not only more mellow dispositions, but also fewer urinal problems. "Fixing" their dogs is just one thing my clients can do to improve their dog's health and ultimately lengthen their lives. The point I want to address in this chapter is some of the more serious ways owners can endanger their own dog's life often without even knowing it. I'm going to break it down into two basic categories: "Indoor and Outdoor" and "Nutrition."

INDOOR AND OUTDOOR

This section deals with a very broad collection of dangerous situations that present themselves mostly in the car, on a walk, or in the house. In the car, the most obvious danger occurs in the summer when even temperatures in the mid-'70s can kill an unattended dog in less than twenty minutes. The sun and car work like a magnifying glass, with your dog serving as the ant. Even on a cool day a simple shift of the sun can cast a dark shadow on your dog's future. Even a simple trip to the post office can turn out to take much longer than originally anticipated, resulting in a game of Russian Roulette with your dog's life.

The car is just one of the places an untimely and unwanted fatality can occur. Many homeowners have a garage they use as a guest room or an additional living space. This may work well during the winter months; however, when summertime hits, any unventilated garage becomes a chamber of death. In any case, a dog should never be left unattended even if just a little while, without access to a generous amount of water. Life is full of the unexpected but we don't want anything happening to our best friend due to an oversight or lack of planning. You should be very nervous when you become the victim of a long line at the supermarket while your dog desperately awaits your arrival back in the car.

What about safety in your vehicle while driving? Dogs should be treated like children under the age of seven. Airbags could be fatal to a dog loose in the front passenger seat due to their size and shape and the fact they're not secured. It's apparent that without a nationally enforced seat belt law for dogs, pet owners will continue to take chances with their dog they would never take with their child.

Getting into an accident while my dog is loose in the car is a chance I just won't take. The safest and most humane way to transport your dog is in the back seat wearing a harness. If the dog is resistant, have someone ride in the back with them initially until the dog feels comfortable wearing it. Since the harness will restrict movement, your dog will feel more secure over time and won't be as tempted to bark at other dogs or jump on your lap while driving. Even the seemingly cruel act of putting your dog in a portable kennel while traveling will prevent your dog from becoming a canine projectile in a collision.

Then there are those long walks through the neighborhood with your loyal friend barefoot and baking on a hot pavement while you enjoy the comfort of rubber-insulated tennis shoes. The walk often happens at the wrong time of the day and for too long at one time. Early morning and sunset are the best times to walk your dog in the hot weather, preferably on dirt or grass. Even sand can heat up very quickly as early as midday.

Another important factor on any walk is how long your dog's legs are when compared to yours. If they're considerably shorter, then you should take that into consideration on long walks, jogs, or bike rides. A miniature poodle can't walk as far as a retriever can before reaching a point of fatigue. Their legs require many more steps to maintain the pace we can sustain with ease.

I was driving through a nearby neighborhood on a summer day a couple of years ago and saw a teenage boy riding a bike while controlling his dog with a leash attached to his bike. The dog was not only a smaller dog but was running while wearing a muzzle, preventing the dog from having any way to perspire. I stopped my car and explained to him how this sweating thing works with dogs. After I explained that he could kill his dog doing this, he removed the muzzle and continued while riding his bike more slowly. Since dogs can only sweat through their tongue, any inadvertent attempt to keep it from hanging out amounts to suffocation for the dog. The additional steps that a smaller dog needs to take amounts to more constant exposure to the prevailing surface temperature. This can result in burning the bottom of your dog's feet.

Even if you properly exercise your dog in more numerous but shorter sessions, they can get dry and cracked foot pads. When I was working dogs on movie sets or on location, a lubricant like Bag Balm was an indispensable item. Just as our hands can get dry and cracked, so too can a dog's feet. Since a good chunk of dog movies involve a dog taking a long journey, the dogs do a lot of running on streets and sidewalks. It's something that should at least be monitored on a semi-regular basis; more if your dog is very active.

Another point to keep in mind is how quickly hard surfaces can heat up on warmer days. Obviously morning is coolest and we don't begin to see temperatures go down until just before sunset. Blacktop surfaces and streets tend to heat up even faster than sidewalks. Metal grates that you pass on the walk can get as hot as a frying pan by noon on a summer day. These are things you must consider when training your dog outdoors or simply walking your dog. When you have your dog on a stay looking at you, is your dog facing the sun when looking at you? Is the dog seemingly not paying attention to avoid the glare or just being stubborn? We always must put ourselves in the place of the dog.

For maximum retention in training, conditions should be optimal and at least comfortable in nontraining situations. I've always feared summer the most when it came to caring for dogs, especially the longer-haired ones. Time isn't your friend on a hot day when everything must come in small doses or not at all. Attempting to train your dog in unfavorable conditions will set a tone of unpleasantness that will carry over to the next lesson. If your dog remembers the last lesson as being uncomfortable, they will begin to anticipate that as being a prevailing condition during training. For this reason, I never train my or my clients' dogs midday in the sun. If you do go out with your dog, try to avoid putting them in a situation where they have to look directly into the sun to respond to your command. Even wind can get in the way of a good outdoor training session. Discomfort should be considered a distraction when it comes to training, as it will lessen your dog's focus and your effectiveness as a trainer.

If you're among the large group of homeowners with a swimming pool, there are a couple of specific rules that apply. The first is that the pool be enclosed, restricting unauthorized access by your dog. However, if you've already violated this rule then the second rule *must* be followed. A dog that could even accidentally tumble into a pool when no humans are in sight is a tragedy waiting to happen. For that reason, this dog needs to be taught to swim whether they like it or not.

It isn't even enough that they know how to swim, but they must also be well versed as to where the pool exit is located. The best way for a dog to learn this is to get them to travel from the shallow end to the steps on their own. How you get your dog into the water varies with each dog. Some will get in willingly, in which case you only have to guide them to the steps. Other dogs can be enticed into the shallow end by you going in with a long leash and enticing them with food or a favorite toy. Then there are those dogs that must be lifted and placed into the shallow end, facing the steps. This is a fairly easy task if you have a small dog, somewhat more difficult with a larger one.

Once they're in the pool and facing the steps, you simply maintain support underneath them with your hand(s) as you guide them out of the pool. You will feel them either swimming on their own or flailing about. Only offer enough support for the dog to avoid going under.

When they reach the top step, praise should be lavished upon them. Behavior that may save their life deserves the highest praise. This should be the only way the dog is ever permitted to exit or enter the pool. Keep rules simple and consistent and confusion will seldom ever come into play. Remember, the goal isn't to create a dog that loves to swim, just one that has no reason to fear it. We want to be prepared for the unexpected in all our safety scenarios and this could be a very crucial one. I could tell you many stories of dogs who were perfectly good swimmers, but drowned as a result of panic and confusion stemming from not knowing how to get out.

Since we've covered the walks, the car, and the pool, let's take a look at some safety techniques that can be exercised *inside* the home. In many respects, they're the same safety measures that would be taken in the presence of a small child.

The first precaution has to do with your dog's tendency—like a small child—to put things in their mouth. You shouldn't offer your dog access to objects that are not food yet are small enough to swallow. This is true with many adult dogs, but almost all puppies. You have to watch out for them attempting to chew on electrical cords or pieces of cloth that can be swallowed and clog up their digestive system. Monitor everything they try to put in their mouth. I'm not opposed to some nibbling on grass or other organic objects, assuming they aren't poisonous or have insecticide on them. I never let dogs have access to *any* man-made product. If it isn't biodegradable, it doesn't belong in your dog's mouth, unless it's a toy. Items like plastic bags, aluminum foil, and other man-made products should be avoided whenever possible.

Supervision is key here. Dogs think a lot like children until both reach the age of four. This isn't conjecture, it's a fact. We need to be constantly aware of what our dog is doing at all times. There's no punishment for bad behavior, just withholding of any reward they would earn for good behavior. We turn learning into earning. We just throw away the bad. Ignore it. Minimize it. Therefore it won't become a game of wills. If your dog thinks you don't care about something, they often lose interest in breaking the rules since no attention is received. Dogs, like children, crave any attention, good or bad.

NUTRITION

When it comes to canine nutrition, the trends are changing rapidly from what they were when I was coming of age. Grain- and corn-based foods are becoming a thing of the past as more and more—mostly purebred—dogs are developing allergies to these foods and their by-products.

Soon I anticipate dogs will be eating a diet similar to the human Keto diet: No grains, no dairy; just "real" food like meat and vegetables. I believe this wasn't a problem back in the day due to less inbreeding of purebred dogs and a smaller number of breeds. The proliferation of dog breeding with many new breeds being introduced has led to a narrowing of the gene pool for many purebred dogs. I can't ever remember mutts ever having food allergies. While I'm not an expert on canine genetics, I certainly see many more "designer" dogs than years ago, when most everyone had a mixed-breed dog.

Staying away from grain and corn is a great way to play it safe. Dogs are omnivores, not carnivores as commonly believed. This means dogs should develop a taste for both meat and vegetables at an early age. Eating habits for dogs are solidified sooner in life than with small children, since they age seven times as fast and get set in their ways relatively early in life.

For this reason, setting the tone early is important; the longer you wait, the harder it will be to establish good nutrition. In addition to the more widely publicized grain and corn prohibition, there are a number of other foods that a dog should never eat.

Pork: There are many dog treats that are pork-flavored yet few of them actually contain pork in its natural form. My grandfather used to tell me at a very young age—and often—how dogs should never eat pork. He said dogs don't digest pork easily and it could cause severe constipation. He seemed to believe it was due to the fact that pigs are also omnivores and had a questionable diet, often including garbage.

Fruit: Fruit isn't recommended for dogs but if you do give them *any* fruit, it is best offered dried. Fresh fruit, especially lemons, oranges, grapefruit, and other "acidic" fruits can give any dog diarrhea. Apples don't contain as much citric acid and tend to be a better bet when it comes to basic fruit. Remove the skin on apples for better digestion. The majority of dried fruit treats found at pet stores are made from apples.

Some fruits that are absolutely prohibited: Grapes and raisins can kill a dog due to the very tight, smooth skin combined with the fact that dogs normally swallow small items like these whole. Dogs simply cannot digest grapes and raisins; giving them even one can result in death. As a general rule, never give produce with a skin to your dog.

Chocolate: I think most dog lovers are aware of the dangers of chocolate. Granted, I've seen dogs digest small doses of milk chocolate with no ill effects. By the same token, a similar sized piece of dark or white chocolate has led many dogs to an emergency vet visit. Your best bet is to stay away from all of it. Every dog reacts differently and small dogs tend to react more dramatically to these forbidden foods.

Bones: We often think of bones and dogs like we think of biscuits and gravy, yet bones can be very dangerous to dogs in certain situations. The first situation is when the bone is too small for the dog based on their size and they attempt to swallow it. It's important that the bone is thick and sturdy like the "knuckle bone" you often see in pet stores or markets.

These bones are proportionately bigger than the dog's throat. They're sturdy and round on the edges. These bones are raw and uncooked. As for cooked bones, they often fragment due to having all the moisture removed, so they can easily splinter and lead your dog to choking. Stay away from giving your dog steak, pork, chicken, or lamb chop bones left over from a human meal. These are not designed for dogs and can be hazardous to their health.

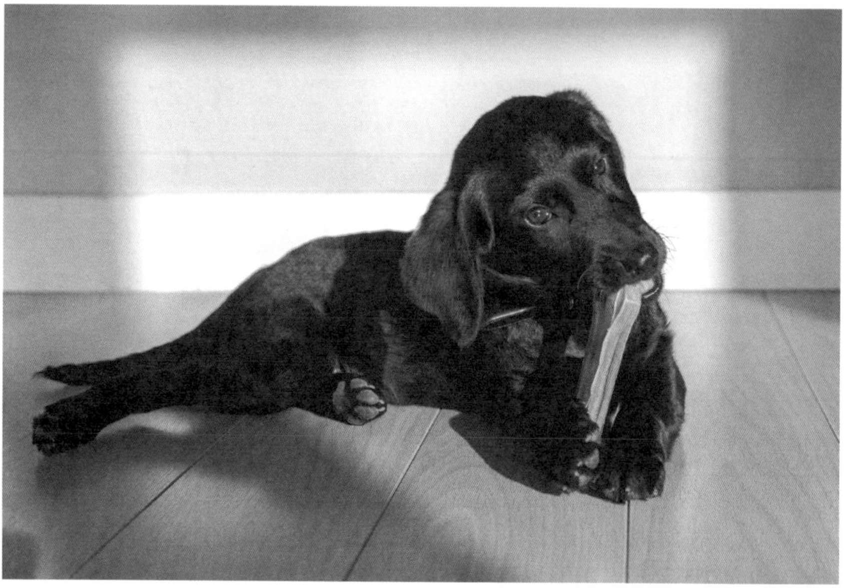

The eye test is the best way to judge what a dog can ingest safely. Dogs can become very obsessive when it comes to bones and will often not stop until it's completely gone. If the bone your dog is chewing looks to be getting dangerously small, you might want to remove and discard it. Since some dogs can be possessive about bones and toys, the best suggestion is to lure them away from it using something very tantalizing, like meat. Show the meat to your dog and toss it away from the bone. Then you'll be able to remove the bone before he can return. Once it's gone, the possessiveness is also gone.

Be careful to properly secure any other food items you don't want your dog to have as well. Just because it's on the sink or table doesn't mean your dog won't attempt to grab it. In fact, you should expect it to happen and secure any food items your dog might attempt to heist. My clients often tell me of thefts their dogs committed in their absence. It only takes a few unsupervised moments for chaos to ensue.

Finally, there is the question of what you should be feeding your dog at mealtime and how often the dog should be fed. A puppy needs a higher protein (puppy diet) which also includes more frequent feedings—as many as three or four times a day. The frequency with which you feed your dog decreases as they grow up. By the time they're four- to six-months old, their feedings can decrease to twice a day. Once they're down to two feedings a day, that can continue for the rest of their life. Feeding only once a day was common fifty years ago, but it will leave your dog feeling either bloated or starved.

My experience feeding a great number of dogs tells me that kibble is not enough. It may deliver the bulk of the nutrition, but it isn't particularly tasty; something I learned from actually eating it as a child.

My collie, Prince, wasn't too picky but I still wanted him to enjoy a tasty, balanced meal. I'll always add something like a spoonful of canned food for flavor. Flavor can be added using chicken broth, gravy, cottage cheese, or anything that enhances flavor in small doses. As I mentioned earlier, I also add something nutritious like vegetables to their meal.

Since kibble is the bulk of most canine meals, preparation is a key element. If your dog willingly eats dry kibble, that's great. The danger lies in allowing your dog to drink large amounts of water afterwards. The kibble in your dog's stomach expands to over twice its original size when combined with water. This can lead to a fatal condition called bloating. Bloat is what happens when the dry food expands beyond the dog's stomach capacity resulting in the stomach twisting. This condition is most prevalent in dogs with large rib cages (Mastiffs, Rottweilers, Shepherds) but it can afflict almost any dog.

I avoid bloat by presoaking the kibble before feeding it. It shouldn't be too soggy; I still want the center of the kibble to be crunchy for dental health. If you do this before feeding you won't have to even consider how much water they drink after their meal. It's all about achieving peace of mind.

This chapter might seem like review for those who have owned many dogs over their lifetime, but a reminder doesn't hurt and it's always better to be safe than sorry. I don't want my readers to learn any of this the hard way. It's my wish to thwart disaster before it presents itself. If you follow these simple guidelines, you will sleep well at night.

A TRIP TO THE VET

If you're bringing a puppy into your home, the vaccination journey begins around three months of age. After the first year, the vaccinations are required less frequently. Adult dogs will typically require boosters periodically.

When meeting with your vet, pay particular attention to the core vaccines. If overlooked, these are the viruses that can pose the greatest health risk to your adult dog or puppy. I advise all dog owners to refrain from taking their dog into community areas until the first two rounds of the Parvovirus shots have been administered. This is probably the most contagious canine disease, primarily transferred by puppies. This shot is typically given now in conjunction with a Canine Coronavirus vaccine.

In addition to staying abreast of each dog's individual immunization schedule, there are a couple of other health concerns that may emerge. Along with viruses, your canine household members should be inspected for parasites.

Giardia is a parasitic infection that affects dogs as well as people. This disease typically originates from a dog or person coming in contact with infected water. It can also be spread by another dog or person carrying the eggs of this parasite. Symptoms of Giardia can include fever, fatigue, and diarrhea.

There are also the more common parasites we encounter in dogs such as worms which actually may vary by state. The most common types are Roundworms, Hookworms, Heartworms, and Whipworms. Here in California we typically only run into Roundworms since the other types are found primarily east of the Rockies. When traveling with dogs to other states, I always make sure I know which types of worms are prevalent in the state I'm visiting. Heartworms are typically the most dangerous, so preventive medicine is normally administered before embarking on a trip. Check with your local veterinarian to determine what type of worming medicine is appropriate if traveling outside of your resident state.

Tapeworms are another type of worm that can infect your dog, but they're typically associated with the presence of fleas and aren't necessarily regional. Always be aware of a dog that's licking or scratching itself, as ingesting fleas can bring about the onset of Tapeworms.

Some of the clearest indicators that a dog has worms are by observing symptoms such as nausea, coughing, and abdominal swelling. A regular inspection of your dog's stool is the easiest way to detect the presence of worms. Dogs with worms will often drag their butt across the ground, believing they can rub them off that way. There are a number of oral medications available at pet stores that specifically address the type of worm you seek to eradicate.

When adding a new dog to your household, the last thing you want to do is bring in a virus or parasite that can infect other canine or feline members already residing in your home. Try to find out as much about the health background of your new household member before bringing them home.

THE CRAZY THINGS MY DOG DOES (AND THE IMPORTANCE OF ACTIVITIES)

I could tell you that all my training sessions involve teaching cool stuff to dogs. I could describe how I'm directing dogs to jump into their owner's arms, run obstacle courses, and retrieve articles—and many times that's been true. Though I often have the luxury of teaching a dog cool tricks, it doesn't comprise the majority of my workday.

Much of what I provide involves behavior modification or reconditioning. Some of a dog's habits are just quirky and don't necessarily lead to a dog being re-homed. On the other hand, other behaviors can be real deal-breakers for owners and could land the dog in a shelter. My job is to eradicate—or at least minimize—all the crazy habits these dogs have developed over time. These habits may have been created by you, the previous owner(s), or even the original breeder. The ease or difficulty in fixing these problems normally lies in how long the problem has existed. Older dogs will typically take longer to reprogram but they can still change as long as they can see and hear. Old dogs can be taught new tricks!

Almost all behavioral problems come from a canine-perceived necessity. A dog that has had to fight for every piece of kibble growing up has learned that battle is the norm. After all, it served its purpose: survival. Some breeders are very fair with their litters and better regulate interaction between littermates. Then there are those who leave the pack to sort it out among themselves. That could lead to a great imbalance. There wouldn't be parity in the litter if pups were left to their own devices. It's survival of the fittest. The regulation by the owner—and the mother of the pups—sets the tone and ensures a level playing field. Those early experiences can mold a dog's disposition as much as anything that occurs later. The good news is the first owner can easily rebuild a runt into a confident, secure dog. First-time owners often accept the blame for their dog's inadequacies but the making of your best friend begins the day the dog is born. It isn't until a dog is about one to two years of age that they leave the formative stage of their mental development—depending on the dog. Note: Puppies that are taken from their mother and littermates sooner than eight to ten weeks tend to have socialization issues with other dogs. My advice is to simply decline the opportunity to take a puppy before they've had sufficient time to socialize with their littermates.

THE CANINE TRIANGLE

My dad often talked about the canine "triangle." The triangle was his way of putting dogs into categories, each represented by one of three corners on a triangle. Each of these three corners are inhabited by dogs that all react differently when put under pressure or cornered. The dogs my dad preferred training for movies normally resided at the top of the pyramid. This is the dog that would resist or fight back when cornered. This is the confident dog. The other two ends of the triangle were occupied by the dog that would attempt to escape and the one that would cower when cornered. Where the dog resides in the triangle can tell you how they should be handled. It also tells you where they most likely ranked among their littermates. The dog at the top of the triangle has probably had things go their way from an early age. The other two dogs may have gotten the short end of the stick and will need to develop that natural confidence through your praise or their own perceived achievements.

Dogs build confidence doing things they fear—with ultimately happy endings.

This positive reinforcement applies to all dogs in all stages of their lives. It's just not as frequently needed with those dogs at the top of the triangle. That's likely what my father meant when he said, "It's easier to slow a fast dog down than to speed up a slow dog." The confident dog doesn't have fear inhibiting them and merely needs to learn control and patience. The timid or jumpy dog needs to learn about trust as previous experiences may have led them to lack confidence in a variety of situations.

It's early human contact that sets the pup on the proper course. A dog that hasn't had early and regular positive contact with people can tend to be aloof or shy toward them later on. Specific abusive experiences with people can lead to that hand-shy dog—or one that bites. They're timid and unsure of themselves in our presence. It creates a canine companion that isn't genuinely as comfortable with humans as they are with other dogs. This dog might be a good play buddy for your other dog, but that doesn't equate to one that truly can appreciate human companionship.

In the absence of that foundation of human touch, the catch-up phase must begin immediately. We have to develop—through praise and food—a trust of all people. This involves having all contact with humans seem wonderful to them. When a person the dog fears is discovered, we must funnel our reward through them. It's like a teeter-totter: We use food and praise to lean the teeter-totter toward the negative. This means that anyone the dog loves now should not feed or reward the dog in the presence of people for which the dog is unsure. It's the same with objects or places. Associating food and praise with those objects and places will change the dog's perception of those situations. Coddling the dog with baby talk when fearful will only validate their fear, whatever or wherever it may exist.

A dog that hasn't had early contact with humans will typically go in one of two directions: Either the dog will be shy, or exceptionally outgoing, even overbearing at times. The overbearing dog may use chewing or leg humping to get what they want: constant attention. My father normally called these behaviors "neurotic" and left it at that. Since I've worked with many more "neurotic" dogs than he did, I find the label very stereotypical. The dogs that chew and hump are trying to get some attention they perceive as missing. Getting attention is one of the ways a dog asserts control. Attention and control go hand in hand. They aren't sure how to express it so it becomes an obsession, like nail biting or pacing in people. The humping is best fixed by using the distraction tool (throw-chain). We would drop it behind them while they're in the act and reward them the moment they stop. Using reward *while* your dog is performing the act would only reinforce the behavior and rewarding them too late would dilute its effectiveness.

The biting of our hands and feet is best solved by either standing (where we always have more power) or by offering an alternative target. Every time they want to bite you, stuff a toy in their mouth. If they drop the toy to bite you again, that would be a good time to intercept their effort with a goody, anything to distract them from you. These behaviors always get worse if you start walking, moving, or using your hands. Movement is the triggering event, so any correction should be done while standing or rising from a sitting position. No evasive measure should be taken. When standing, you'll always be in a more powerful position, regardless of what correction is needed.

The shy dog will show their frustration in ways we may not recognize. The behavior displayed may emerge immediately or later on as a triggering event occurs. A perfect example is the dog that has a visiting canine in their house. The resident dog, though perfectly housetrained, may decide to strategically pee in places frequented by the visiting dog. Until corrected (using a distraction tool) or the scent dissipates, your dog's marking could continue even long after the other dog has left the house.

Separation anxiety can often trigger rogue destruction in the house by both the shy and outgoing dog. The signs of this are chewed baseboards or damaged furniture, among other things. Dogs don't normally damage items they deem necessary to their future. The objects of their anxiety tend to be items valued more by us than them. This subtle form of rebellion can also appear in the form of strategic peeing. This tinkling will usually occur near the door through which their favorite people exit and enter. This simply demonstrates that it's the act of leaving that's triggering the behavior. This means a reward should be associated with leaving them alone, even if you're only going out for the mail.

Where the home violation occurs can tell you a lot about what's triggering the dog's behavior. For instance, a dog that chews your personal items is probably upset at you specifically for some perceived neglect. What we view as "getting stuff done" is interpreted by dogs as indifference if they don't feel involved. This is a huge factor in why many dogs test their owner's training while they're on the phone or talking to someone else. They're trying to remain the center of our attention. Rather than simply giving the dog long periods of attention, we give them attention only for things that are pleasing to us. Awarding praise in the absence of real achievement lessens the effect of praise whether with a food reward or verbally. Dogs tend to be more passive in exacting their message when they feel ignored. Nearly every canine act is due to their own real perceived need. Very little of it is random.

Since we know these rebellious acts aren't random, we need to make a habit of compensating the dog. This compensation can appear in the form of offering something they value after enduring our periods of personal preoccupation. This lets them know that there *is* a way to get what they want—by waiting. Much like people, dogs don't generally value things too easily acquired. If you're consistent in rewarding them at the end of any long wait, whether on a "stay" or not, you'll be providing something that's important to them.

Another valuable reward for your dog could be playing with them. This could involve tugging on a towel or playing with a toy. It's a very important part of a dog's life. However, much like swimming, all dogs don't naturally like to do it. If they do, that's great. If not, then they need to be taught, much like walking on leash. When the dog is satisfying their own need, they're less concerned about what we are doing. This leads to your dog being less obnoxious when they're bored as they know their time with you will come. It's the getting nothing part that encourages their bad behavior while idle.

If your dog has a favorite toy, you shouldn't let them play with it all the time. This could lead to a dog that becomes bored with it—or obsessive with it. I see many clients whose dogs either never play with their toys or have one toy they obsess and whine over. Too much of anything is a bad thing. Walks shouldn't be too long and the play time too frequent. Both should be used sparingly and in conjunction with reward. Favorite toys—or food—shouldn't be brought to public dog parks, as this can create a scuffle between your dog and another who is bored or possessive.

Sometimes you have to be creative in getting a dog to play. When I was a small boy, my dad always encouraged me to teach his movie dogs to "pad." You might know this as "tug-of-war." The first time I was asked to do this, I would take the designated dog to a place where there were no other dogs or people. It could be the yard or my own bedroom. I would then find something like a sock. Sometimes I could get a dog to play with it by teasing them to grab it—and then immediately letting them win. If that failed, I would put a piece of hot dog inside the sock and knot the opening at the top. Then I'd poke a small hole in the bottom so the dog could really smell what's inside. This made any dog with a good appetite crazy and normally resulted in an enthusiastic round of tug-of-war. Every play session always ended with the dog winning the battle and getting the reward inside. Whenever the dog seemed ready to stop playing, I would let them win and praise them. I never gave them food myself; it always came from the sock. Once the dog had mastered tugging with the hot dog inside, I removed the hot dog using the same sock. Eventually I could use a new unscented sock, and induce a great play session without using any food.

This is just one example of how you can encourage your dog to play. It can never be forced, but the art of teaching it lies in the teasing aspect. There's a playful urgency to draw our dog to our object, whether it's a ball or a sock. The teasing is what gets the dog interested. When the dog makes their first attempt to grab the object, we allow them to and praise them lavishly. Repeating this routine will result in a dog that doesn't need to win as much as they simply enjoy doing it. The earlier you can teach your dog to play, the less likely they are to use your arms or legs as chew toys. It's much easier to redirect bad behavior than it is to eliminate the behavior, especially in our younger canine students.

Search for the object your dog gravitates toward right away. It will be different for every dog. Some dogs will not like hard toys. Some dogs won't like anything heavy, or certain fabrics. It's just part of the learning process we all must endure with any new dog early in our relationships. An open mind is your greatest weapon and will help you avoid mistakes based on previous information—or misinformation. Just because something never happened with your previous dogs doesn't mean it won't happen now. I still run into situations I've never run into previously and each time it prepares me for the next "fluke" dog I encounter. I see new, bizarre behaviors all the time.

Many relocated dogs—mutt and purebred alike—are being placed in shelters and new homes because of some specific bad behavior. That behavior could be barking, destruction of the house, escaping the yard, or aggression toward any number of things, living or nonliving. There's no amount of yelling or physical correction that's going to solve a problem the dog has chosen themselves. The key to getting rid of the behavior is to take away their perceived payoff for doing it.

Every dog has their own distinct payoff. Sometimes the payoff is simply the reaction it gets from you. If you display anger after the behavior, your outburst may represent more attention than they had received prior to performing that behavior. Attention is a huge payoff for a dog and is the least costly for you to provide. Even an occasional momentary acknowledgment can satisfy a dog.

Then there's the most obvious reward, which could include any number of things. It could be a walk or a play session. It could be food or praise. Every dog is motivated in different ways. Most of the dogs I work with care more about the walk than the food. I tell my clients that a dog will never bite the hand of the person who walks them. A walk often represents the ultimate payoff.

Determining your dog's personal payoff is the key to providing the most meaningful reward. The key to solving many of their behavior issues is in determining what your dog finds important. What will they receive? Can they trust you to consistently acknowledge their stellar performance? Discipline for poor behavior is often dispensed more consistently than praise is given for good behavior. Keep both balanced.

Try to involve your dog in as much healthy activity as possible. The art of play is an acquired skill. It should be initiated by you as much as possible. If your dog initiates play, I will ask them to do something else for me first—this could be any simple activity like "Sit." This way I'm taking control away from the dog temporarily. Upon completion of my task, I will give the reins back to them. This way play becomes my idea, not theirs.

Play can make a big difference in reprogramming your dog's obsessive behavior. It's creating balance, like a balanced diet. Rather than focusing all their energy on one thing—like humping our leg—we're introducing them to alternative methods of venting their frustration. We aren't saying "no" to one thing as much as we are saying "yes" to another thing. If you had to go through the day of an average domestic dog, you might find yourself less than satisfied. If we don't help discover productive activities for our dog, they will initiate their own destructive habits.

Dogs are naturally resourceful and often resist having their natural spirit stifled. When we're more attentive to their needs, we tend to receive a large return. The dog that is understood doesn't need to make misbehavior their voice. It's our task to give them the tools to communicate properly. Every dog deserves that.

WHEN IT'S TIME TO SAY GOODBYE

Even dogs given the best of care will make trips to the vet for their canine ailments. One of those trips will be the last, as the dog must mercifully be put down. Some dogs die early due to accidents, while others live well beyond their life expectancy. But someday you will have to face the reality that your best friend's life has come to its end.

How do you know when that time has come? Assuming they are not in pain, this is my basic barometer for senior dogs. My criteria for feeling good about their continued existence is that they can still go to the bathroom, they still have an appetite, and can get from point A to point B by themselves. If they can do all these seemingly simple tasks, then no guilt should be derived from keeping them around. These elderly dogs won't typically express pain outwardly, so look for a dog that pants constantly, which is one of the more common and subtle ways a dog expresses discomfort.

Too many times, we keep our dogs around because we can't bear the thought of losing them. Though it comes from the right place, this can be a very selfish act. It's easy for us to make a decision based on our own comfort level since dogs don't always express their pain to us. It's all about quality of life. If it's a life you wouldn't want to endure yourself, why would you want that same low standard of life for your dog? The ultimate act of love is recognizing when your dog is no longer living the life you would want for yourself.

When the time has come to let your dog go, how then do you cope with the grief?

In my life, I've dealt with the loss of hundreds of dogs. Some were dogs I grew up with. Some were dogs my dad had as part of his business. Then there were the dogs I trained for other animal suppliers and dogs belonging to my private training clients. I was attached to them all. However, nothing hurts worse than losing your own dog. Unlike many family members and friends, your dog was always there for you. They never judged you, laughed at you, or put their needs ahead of yours. They were committed to you; not merely involved.

Pet owners often add another companion animal to benefit their first dog. Their goal is for the dog to be less lonely, but I'm here to tell you there's a much greater purpose to having that second dog: It will make the eventual loss of the first dog easier to bear. When we have another dog we can talk to them, cry on them, and shower them with the attention we wish we could still give to our deceased pet. I'm not saying to go get another dog simply to prepare for the future. Another dog would obviously require more time and space than many pet owners can give. A dog should only be acquired to meet your needs, not the imagined needs of your existing dog.

The best advice I can give is similar to any advice given regarding the loss of any family member. It's always best to think back rather than forward. Think of the things your dog has given you and what you've given them. And if you still have your canine companion, enjoy each day and live for the moment with your dog because tomorrow is never guaranteed for any of us.

A FINAL WORD

I hope this book has given you the insight on how I feel toward dogs. My goal has been to give you not only the "how" but also the "why." The question of "why" was the only one that really mattered growing up. It just wasn't enough for me to see the end result—I wanted to know what the dogs were thinking. I was a very curious only child. Having no siblings left me with a lot of time to experiment with our numerous canine tenants.

Before I ever became a professional trainer I "manipulated" dogs. I learned how to induce canine behavior by behaving a certain way myself. Dogs will always believe in you until you betray them. Even then, they're far more forgiving than humans.

In your training, be consistent. Whatever rules you implement in the beginning should remain valid. Dogs don't believe in gray areas. Be firm. Giving your dog an inch now will most certainly result in them taking a mile later. Be humane. Treat your dog the way you'd want to be treated if the roles were reversed.

If you follow these simple rules, you'll not only achieve the success you want, but you'll feel good about the process. It's not just about the training, but also the methods. If you enjoy the journey, you will better appreciate the destination. Hopefully you have enjoyed your training journey with me and will find applying this knowledge a joyful experience.

You best friend deserves an owner who truly understands them. It's your insight that will bring calmness to your dog as they don't have to misbehave to be understood. In my opinion, dogs are the most interesting beings on earth. They see things the way we did as children. There's no rationalizing with a dog. They see the world with an innocence we can only remember.

Remember to keep things simple with your canine companion. Never expect them to read your mind. If you desire something of them, just tell them. There isn't any sense training your dog if you're not going to use the commands you've taught them. Training will teach you things about your best friend that you would never have discovered in the absence of it. Open that treasure chest and find the jewels that await the educated owner. Dogs want to be trained for one simple reason: It gives them the ability to please you more often. Pleasing each other is really what training your best friend is all about.

Now that you know the words, the next step is simply applying what you've learned. Success in dog training is when information and application meet. One without the other will never be mastered. Each time we encounter an issue, our skills expand and they can be used on our next dog, and so on. Keep practicing and never be afraid of an uncomfortable situation with your dog. One day you'll look back and say, "I've dealt with this hundreds of times, no problem." That's when you'll know this book has made a difference.

GLOSSARY OF DOG TRAINING TERMS

Bridge: The moment when good canine behavior is achieved while the dog is simultaneously fed or receiving verbal or physical praise from the owner or trainer.

Decompression: The mannerisms shown by a dog that is gradually becoming acclimated to a situation. These mannerisms can be demonstrated through panting, yawning, barking, or whining.

Desensitization: The act of inducing a dog to endure an uncomfortable situation in order to change its connotation of that scenario. It's leading a dog to learn that present positive experiences can dilute or eliminate previously existing negative canine recollections. The quote "What doesn't kill you makes you stronger" is the layman's explanation.

Distraction: Using noise, physical contact, or vibrations to redirect, to eventually eliminate poor canine behavior. It's an alternative to physical correction. Distraction should always be applied during moments of mischief. Praise is applied immediately upon the succession of bad behavior. The moment they receive praise could be called "The Bridge."

Empowerment: When undesirable behavior is rewarded rather than given minimal importance. It is the application of either food reward or verbal/physical praise when current canine behavior actually calls for distraction or mild correction. It becomes—through regular use—a method of transferring insecurity from the owner/trainer to his or her canine pupil.

Exposure: Often referred to as "putting the dog in the stands." It's the act of regularly placing your dog in situations new to him or her. It's the systematic relocation of your dog while making each experience or new location fondly remembered. Calmness is eventually achieved by administering praise or food in situations where a dog may initially feel uncomfortable—molding canine calmness in similar situations moving forward.

Going Deep: Putting your dog in a challenging training position and welcoming their mistakes.

Mark: A designated location where a dog will be expected to stay. This mark could take the form of a patch of grass, doorstep, carpet, driveway, etc. The mark is a physical boundary that a dog can clearly define by its texture, color, or elevation. The dog recognizes the boundary either visually or with their front feet.

Payoff: What a dog gains (in their mind) by participating in any type of behavior, good or bad. "What's in it for the dog?" Payoff is what a dog expects to happen when they behave or misbehave. They could be well-behaved for positive attention, or be poorly behaved for *any* attention. It's important that your dog's good behavior doesn't receive less attention than their mischief.

Putting Them in the Stands: Subjecting your dog to something they fear (from a safe distance) rather than retreating from it.

Separation Anxiety: The insecurity a dog feels in the absence of our presence. It's the feeling of uncertainty a dog gets when they haven't been gradually accustomed to our absence. Often the potential existence of Separation Anxiety makes a case for crate training early in a dog's life. Early crate training gives the dog security in confinement rather than a feeling of imprisonment. The uncertainty of not knowing what to do or where to be in your absence can lead to destruction and mischief.

Trigger: The thing or event that brings out the worst in a dog. The trigger normally leads to timid or aggressive behavior. The trigger could be another dog, a new person, a motorcycle, or any number of common objects or situations. When we know what triggers our dog, we can eradicate the resulting bad behavior.

DOGS BY GROUP

The rating system below is based on my own personal experience working with most of these breeds during my long dog training career. Another experienced dog lover may form his or her own rating system based on *their* life experiences with different breeds. You will notice that most of my ratings are quite broad due to the diversity of each collective canine group. This rating system is simply designed to give you a preliminary guide to finding the right dog for *you*.

THE SPORTING DOGS

Spaniels: These high-energy hunting breeds include the Cocker Spaniel, the Clumber Spaniel, the Springer Spaniel, the Water Spaniel, the Brittany Spaniel, and the Pointer. Outside of the Pointer, these dogs all would be considered among the smaller breeds. Their energy rating ranges from five to seven.

Setters: These larger sporting dogs include the Irish, English, and Gordon Setters. Their energy rating ranges from six to eight.

Retrievers: These more popular larger dogs are renowned water dogs. They're also known for their soft bite. This group includes the Golden, Labrador, Flat-Coated, Curly Coated, and Chesapeake Retrievers. The energy range is broad with this group; somewhere between four and eight.

European Sporting Utility Dogs: This hearty hunting group includes the German Shorthaired Pointer, the Vizsla, the Weimaraner, and the Wirehaired Pointing Griffon. These are high-energy sporting breeds with a range between seven and nine.

THE HOUNDS

These dogs could be considered a subsection of the Sporting Group. The most common breeds are Greyhound, Basset Hound, Bloodhound, Dachshund, and the Beagle. But the group is broad and includes the Harrier, Scottish Deerhound, American Foxhound, Whippet, Irish Wolfhound, Borzoi, English Foxhound, Otterhound, Norwegian Elkhound, Afghan, Saluki, Basenji, Coonhound, Rhodesian Ridgeback, and the Ibizan hound. Many of the smaller hounds, like the Dachshund, Beagle, and Basenji can be around six to eight on the energy scale. The larger breeds like Bloodhound and Rhodesian Ridgeback tend to be a little lower on the scale, but their size can be an equalizer.

THE WORKING DOGS

These dogs are used most commonly as police, guard, and/or protection dogs. They are a vast group that includes the Boxer, German Shepherd, Doberman Pinscher, Great Pyrenees, Rottweiler, and the Standard and Giant Schnauzers. These breeds all can range from eight to ten on the energy scale. The Belgian Malinois, a newer addition to the American Kennel Club (AKC) scene, would receive maybe the highest number of any breed mentioned. They are nearly all tens on the scale.

THE DRAFT DOGS

While these dogs are considered "working dogs," they fall under the subcategory of "draft dogs." This family of dogs includes the Alaskan Malamute, The Siberian Husky, Bernese Mountain Dog, and the Samoyed. These dogs tend to be very independent and all are near the top of the energy spectrum.

THE RESCUE DOGS

This group is also a subset of the working dogs. The prominent members of this group are the Newfoundland and the St. Bernard. These dogs are around six on the energy scale, but their size can make that number seem higher.

OTHER WORKING DOGS

This category covers dogs whose roles as working dogs are much less specific; historically serving in some "sentry" capacity. This group includes the Akita, Bullmastiff, Great Dane, Komondor, and the Kuvasz.

THE TERRIER GROUP

This group of dogs resides near the top of the energy scale, even though many of the breeds are quite small. They're broken down into two categories: Short-legged and Long-legged.

The short-legged breeds include the Australian Terrier, Cairn Terrier, and the Norwich, Norfolk, and Scottish Terriers. Other members are the West Highland Terrier, Skye Terrier, Dandie Dinmont Terrier, and the Sealyham Terrier. It's possible that one of the newest members—the Jack Russell Terrier—tends to possess the highest energy of this entire group, all the way up to nine or ten. The long-legged Terriers include the Airedale Terrier, American Staffordshire Terrier, and the American Pit Bull Terrier. Additional members include the Border Terrier, Bedlington Terrier, Bull Terrier, Fox Terrier, Welsh Terrier, and the Wheaton Terrier. This group tends to be a larger version of the short-legged versions. They occupy the top two notches of the scale in general.

THE HERDING DOGS

Lassie and her Collie relatives belong to this group. Their herding objects are mostly sheep and cattle. German Shepherds can be included in this group as well as the working dog group. Other entries in this class are the Old English Sheepdog, Bearded Collie, Welsh Corgi, and Shetland Sheepdog. Also included here are the Australian Cattle Dog, the Bouvier, the Briard, and the Puli. There are also the three Belgians: the Belgian Sheepdog, the Belgian Tervuren, and the Belgian Malinois. I consider the Malinois and German Shepherd to belong to the working group, but historically these two breeds were considered herding dogs. Excluding the Shepherd and Malinois, this group runs around six to eight on the energy scale. They all tend to be larger breeds. Their herding abilities lead them to be quite protective yet typically good with children and other dogs.

NONWORKING BREEDS

I consider this group to include miscellaneous dogs. These dogs aren't specifically assigned to any broad category. Many of them once were considered working dogs but since coming to America, their roles have changed. Most of these breeds are now merely companion dogs. There are two categories: Toy and Non-sporting.

TOY BREEDS

These breeds typically have a small bite but a big bark. Their roster begins with a few Asian entries: The English Toy Spaniel, Japanese Chin, Papillon, Pekingese, Pugs, and the Shih Tzu. Other entrants include the Toy Poodle, Pomeranian, Yorkshire Terrier, Manchester Terrier, Miniature Pinscher, Silky Terrier, Italian Greyhoud, Brussels Griffon, Affenpinscher, and the Maltese. I would place these dogs somewhere on the scale between five and ten range since so many different breeds reside in this group.

NONSPORTING GROUP

This group looks a lot like their Toy counterparts and their energy rating is similar. This group includes the Standard Poodle, Bichon Frise, Lhasa Apso, Tibetan Terrier, Dalmatian, Schipperke, Keeshond,

Chow Chow, French Bulldog, English Bulldog, and the Boston Terrier. The history of this group doesn't suggest any previous role in serving man other than companionship.

ACKNOWLEDGMENTS

I'd like to thank the following people for their support in my life and as a dog trainer.

My mom, Linda Jean Weatherwax (now Linda Jean Lackie), for supporting my efforts as a writer long before I ever touched a typewriter. She has been behind me every step of the way.

My great uncles, Jack and Frank Weatherwax. Like their brother Rudd, they trained dogs for film. While working for Carl Spitz, Jack trained "Toto" for *The Wizard of Oz*. Frank's best-known movie dog was "Spike," who starred in *Old Yeller* and *A Dog of Flanders*. Frank also helped Rudd run his dog supply business, The Hollywood Dog Training School. He played a large role in training the original Lassie, "Pal." Dog training runs deep in our family.

John Lovins, my lifelong friend and also a writer. Thanks for inspiring me to turn an idea into a book.

Nick Harrison, my literary agent, the man who played the most significant part in finding a home for my book. I couldn't have done this without him.

My publisher, Skyhorse Publishing, and my editor, Leah Zarra. Thanks for taking a chance on this first-time author.

William S. Grisco, friend of over four decades and talented movie trainer who knows what it's like to have to fill the shoes of an accomplished movie-training dad. His father and mine were once business partners when Weatherwax Trained Dogs was first founded in 1976.

Well-known author Ace Collins, the man who provided the beautiful Collie gracing the cover of this book. He is the author of *Lassie: A Dog's Life, The First Fifty Years.*

Radio host Dr. Laura Schlessinger, someone I've worked with and learned from. I often see a parallel between her child-raising mentality and my dog training style.

My daughters, Jean and Brooke, for serving as my part-time dog training assistants for over three decades collectively.

My Dog Training Mentors—My wonderful grandfather, Rudd B. Weatherwax, the dog training pioneer who cowrote *The Story of Lassie: His Discovery and Training from Puppyhood to Stardom* with John H. Rothwell, published by W. H. Allen in 1950. He also *cowrote The Lassie Method: Raising & Training Your Dog with Patience, Firmness & Love* in 1971. Robert Weatherwax, my accomplished dog training father who produced The Lassie Dog Training System (VHS 1990). He was assisted by both Carol Riggins and myself in the making of the video filmed at the Disney Ranch in Santa Clarita. The fabulous dog trainer Karl Miller whose fundamentals I use in my everyday training. Next to my father and grandfather, his influence looms the largest in my overall style. Richard Calkins and Steven Ritt, both top trainers at my father's company, who helped me acquire my earliest experience working on a movie set as their training assistant.

The Photographers—Don Lackie, my stepfather, who took the pictures that helped sell my book. He expertly photographed three different dogs in this book. Christopher Zsarnay, the man responsible for capturing the wonderful images of Zoey, the King Charles Spaniel featured in this book. Jennifer Lux, the talented wife of one of my best friends. Her photos of Socket were nothing short of magical.

The Weatherwax Way Dogs—Prince, the tenth-generation descendant of the original Lassie. Sadly, Prince passed shortly before this book was sold. He appears with me in the author photo on the back cover. Magnum, the beautiful German Shepherd owned by my friend and former dog training client, Michelle Fine. Zoey, a tri-colored King Charles Spaniel owned by Christopher and Lois Szarnay; also my former clients. Buddy, the English Bulldog owned by good friend Deborah Moynier. Socket, the Bernese Mountain Dog/Golden

Retriever mix owned by my longtime friend Harrison Lux and his talented wife, Jennifer. Riley, a white Terripoo owned by Don and Linda Lackie. Riley was the longtime playmate of the late Prince. Riley was a rescue from the West Valley Animal Shelter.

INDEX